IT'S
NOT
ME,
IT'S
YOU

ALSO BY JOHN KIM

I Used to Be a Miserable F*ck

Single. On Purpose.

IT'S NOT ME, IT'S YOU

Break the
Blame Cycle.
Relationship
Better.

JOHN KIM
VANESSA BENNETT

HarperOne
An Imprint of HarperCollins*Publishers*

HarperCollins books may be purchased for educational, business, or sales promotional use. For information, please email the Special Markets Department at SPsales@harpercollins.com.

FIRST EDITION

Art by Isaac Zakar/Shutterstock, Inc.

Library of Congress Cataloging-in-Publication Data is available upon request.

ISBN 978-0-06-320631-1
ISBN 978-0-06-328675-7 (Intl)

22 23 24 25 26 LSC 10 9 8 7 6 5 4 3 2 1

The names and identifying characteristics of some individuals in this book have been changed to protect their privacy.

Contents

PART 3   Build Something Sustainable

Vanessa,

Thank you for supporting me, challenging me, and holding up a mirror. For giving me a new kind of love experience that opens fists and creates new definitions. For holding my hand through the dark and my face in the light. For doing life with me. Not at me. Or around me. For watching *The Golden Girls* with me as I fall asleep, squeezing my morning wood (not in a sexual way but in an "I love you now get the fuck up" way), accepting my inappropriateness, proofreading all my shit, and scratching my back when I know it grosses you out. For being my partner, my friend, my confidant and copilot on this crazy thing called life.

John,

You remain one of my greatest "knowings." I appreciate you and all that you are and that you do, for me, for us, for Logan. Thank you for challenging my definitions of what a relationship could look and feel like. Thank you for teaching me that we can accept responsibility for how we've messed up and that it doesn't mean we are "bad." Thank you for giving me consistency and showing me that real love is calm and patient. Thank you for championing me, my story, and my future. With you, I feel both held and free, and as Thich Nhat Hanh says, that is the real way to love and feel loved.

Authors' Note

There's a popular daytime talk show where the host, a relationship therapist, grabs his wife's hand from the audience at the end of the show, and together they strut down the runway as if they are disappearing into an imaginary sunset. And giving the impression that, when it comes to a picture-perfect relationship, they are the experts and this is where you *need* to be if your own relationship is fraught with challenges, difficulties, and struggles. If only you were more like them, you too could strut down a runway with your beau in perfect loving bliss every day.

As therapists, we can tell you, that show irks the shit out of us.

We were hesitant to write this book. We didn't want to be like that slightly arrogant talk-show host couple—"experts" wagging fingers or telling people what a healthy relationship "should" look like. We also realized that the only way to truly help someone picking up a book looking for relationship advice was to be brutally honest about the state of our own relationship. Which would mean, instead of grabbing each other's hand and walking off into a sunset, sitting down on the couch across from you and telling you our deepest and darkest secrets, not the other way around (which is what we're used to).

The truth is, every relationship is different. No relationship is perfect. There isn't a "one size fits all." Our own relationship is far from perfect, even though we're both therapists who specialize in relationships and are probably the most qualified people to "get it right" when it comes to love.

We may have the kinds of credentials that would make for a perfect union, but we, like you, are flawed and complicated humans. We have both learned and grown through many other failed relationships and are committed to putting that learning to work in our relationship with each other. Even then, our relationship doesn't always make for easy breezy days of perfect communication and mind-blowing sex and a rom-com-level daily love story. In short, even two people who have all the tools and knowledge and 10,000 hours of relationship skill sets, who are best suited to that "perfect" relationship you might be seeking, have arguments, miscommunications, expectations that ruin the moment, pasts that ruin the future, competing love languages, different ways of cleaning, exercising, eating, and parenting—and the list goes on and on.

We wrote this book together in hopes that by pulling the curtain back and exploring our own real issues and how we manage them, as well as stories and learnings from clients over the years, we can help you with your relationship. We have learned and continue to learn from examining our past, showing up and holding ourselves accountable in our present, and working toward a common goal in the future: continued expansion, a deepening of intimacy, and a more solid connection and relationship with Self. This book is not us telling you how to do something. It's you seeing yourself in someone else's story and then gaining insight and tools to maybe try again in your own life, or to approach it differently this time.

> **Self:** When capitalized, a reference to "the totality of one's being," according to Carl Jung.

This book is not about Mars versus Venus. It's not about gender or age or whether you're married, engaged, or even monogamous. It's about relationship dynamics. It doesn't matter what your relationship structure is or what it looks like from the outside. It's more about how you want it to feel on the inside.

We have all read the relationship self-help books that feel a bit detached. They might claim to give us "tools," but they feel clinical, like the author is looking at us over the rim of their glasses while telling us how we "should" be in order to get it "right." We've also all read the books by non-experts. They might give us a lot of personal insight and advice, but when none of the growth and change of many couples is tracked or practiced over the long term, it's hard to guarantee that what worked for one couple will work for you. Because, let's face it, there is a fair amount of credibility in something that has been researched to death, involving couples who show up and do the work and stay together long enough to know these practices really help.

We wanted this book to be a combination of both approaches. We have the knowledge and understanding of the research and the theories, and we have seen what works and what does not work with hundreds, if not thousands, of clients. But we are also human, with stories and baggage and traumas of our own. We are two people who struggle day to day to show up, be vulnerable, stay connected and committed, all while raising a kid in today's crazy world. We just happen to also be therapists.

Love is its own living breathing thing. It is formless, and there is no owner's manual. We are all constantly learning, growing, and evolving and holding it all together as best we can.

—John and Vanessa

PART 1

Survive the Collision

Introduction:
The American Nightmare

The most common reason our clients end up working with us can be traced back to a single story, what we call the American Nightmare.

The Norman Rockwell painting:

Jack meets Diane at an early age. (We're using stereotypically male and female names, but we've seen this story play out with many different relationship dynamics.) Maybe in high school or college or in their early twenties. The collision is powerful. Each believes they found their "one." Now life can really begin. So they run toward the picket fence as fast as they can. Get married, have kids, buy a hybrid SUV. Because that's what happy looks like, right? That's the American Dream. Looking into each other's eyes, wrapped in love as they stand in front of their brand-new home, bought with a high-interest loan because today it's next to impossible to save for a down payment *and* maintain good credit. His hand on her stomach reveals that they are expecting. This becomes their Facebook cover photo. Then reality hits. Bills and diapers and everything required to start adulting.

That is not the nightmare, though most people think it is. That's just a painting traced by the blueprint passed down from our parents combined with the cold realities of raising children and having a mortgage that nobody ever really talks about. We know this painting very well. It's the one we ripped down when our parents and/or society hung it in our living room without our conscious permission. So we think the American Nightmare doesn't apply to us. We know the picket fence has splinters, so maybe we try to go a different way.

In our generation's version of the story, Diane spends her twenties exploring her sexuality and new drugs to connect to her spiritual self and Jack works smarter not harder as he builds multiple start-ups instead of climbing a single corporate ladder. They meet in their thirties on a dating app and quickly have a kid because fertility windows are closing. Or Jack and Diane meet in their late teens and decide *not* to have kids, and instead of moving to the suburbs they buy a loft downtown and settle into a pattern of coexistence where, instead of exchanging vows, they open their relationship and exchange partners.

Many end up on our "couch" thinking they avoided the nightmare because they didn't follow their parents' path or the traditional one. But they end up in the therapy room all the same. Because the nightmare isn't produced by kids or houses or corner offices or marriage. It doesn't matter what type of blueprint you're tracing. The nightmare is produced by what's underneath the painting. Not being taught how to have healthy relationships. Not knowing about attachment styles and their impact on relationships. Having no clue about different love languages, codependency, and the importance of not repeating patterns. No one taught us that the lightning in the bottle may actually be dysfunction, not "chemistry." We never learn how to create a safe space, communicate effectively, and fight without fighting.

So we push things down. Pretend. Run. Hide. Numb. Then one day we wake up and realize we're not happy. Now we're processing our anger in couples counseling. We're not doing any work. We're just going through the motions because we don't want to be the bad guy. Or it's too late. We have drifted too far to turn back. It's not just about learning new tools for forgiveness at this point. Feelings have permanently changed. We believe we're with the wrong person. We want out.

Diane has outgrown Jack. Or Jack may already be getting his emotional (and/or physical) needs met by someone else. Now comes divorce. At first it's freeing. Then reality hits again. Being single is hard, especially if you have kids. Also, we're not in our twenties anymore. Add the internal ticking clock and today's toxic dating swipe culture and we can start to feel hopeless. Old. Left behind. We can start to internalize and believe that we are less than or defective. Or we compromise and get together with anyone who comes our way so we don't have to be alone. And the same patterns keep happening. We are still in the nightmare because we haven't done any real work on ourselves.

Now Jack and Diane are in their late thirties, forties, maybe fifties, depending on how many more relationships they went through without going on any kind of inner journey or awakening. Then one day it hits them. Maybe at a coffee shop as they overhear a young couple assassinating each other's character just like they used to do. They know how that's going to end. Or maybe it hits them on the bathroom floor after a long sleepless night crying over another breakup. Either way, they're done. They know they need to change. They can't do this anymore. They've lost something valuable. Not just time, but their relationship with themselves. They've hit rock bottom. And *this* is when we get the call, the email, the DM.

Finally, they are willing to look inward and work on themselves. Finally, they really want to learn about relationship dynamics and their unhealthy patterns, to look at their story and wiring, to heal old wounds. Finally, they are willing to attend Al-Anon meetings, read self-help books instead of just buying them, and see a therapist on more than an "as needed" basis. Finally, they have a real chance at building something sustainable, meaningful, and lasting. Finally, they are working on their relationship with themselves. Finally, they have awakened from the nightmare.

This isn't just what happens to most of our clients. It's what happened to us. We went through a version of this ourselves. Neither of us had kids or tree swings, but we have both been married and divorced, engaged and broken it off, chased the dream instead of examining the blue-print underneath it. We loved hard and recklessly and learned that intensity and passion aren't enough to build and sustain a relationship. We lost ourselves, but it wasn't our fault. No one taught us how to have healthy relation-ships. We learned like everyone else: through what we saw growing up—advertising, movies—and through lots of pain. Through stuffing feelings down. Reacting instead of responding. Not having healthy boundaries or building a strong sense of self. Not knowing how to communicate. Not having the ability to take ownership or create safe spaces. Seeking validation and approval. Getting into things way too fast. Not spotting (or paying attention to) red flags. Not knowing how to be alone. We ran. Hid. And numbed.

And that's why we wrote this book.

It took us many relationships, our own inner self journey (which we're still on), therapy, therapy school, and experi-ence helping thousands of people with their relationships to learn to have better ones ourselves. Vanessa woke up at thirty-one, after ending an engagement and moving from New York to Los Angeles to start over. I thought I woke up at thirty-five, after my divorce. But I really didn't wake up until forty. I had to go through a few more relationships with low awareness, repeating old unhealthy patterns.

This book is the accumulation of our own personal love lessons as well as what we learned working with clients in our therapy practices. It's everything we wish we knew when we were younger. Because, if we had, we would have woken up from the nightmare a lot sooner.

Let's end this section by setting some expectations and clearing up a few more things. We've said it already and we will repeat it a few more times, maybe a lot more times. We are not perfect. We struggle. Sometimes (a lot of times) we fall back into old patterns. But we keep showing up, over and over, to learn from what happened and then try again. We turn things over and inspect them from all sides, own what is ours, and then recommit to the work.

We are also not married. We aren't against the idea of marriage. John has been married before, and Vanessa has been engaged. We just don't see marriage as something necessary at this stage of our lives. For both of us, marriage in the past felt like an arbitrary contract. One in which "I am committed to you forever and you are committed to me" didn't mean "I'm going to grow, take care of myself, take responsibility, heal my old wounds, and work to build and foster something thriving and sustainable with you." Or marriage was something that the other person felt was what we "had" to do because it's what everyone else did, or because it was what would make the other person feel that we were really committing to them and that it would somehow magically relieve their (or our) deep-rooted fear of abandonment and unlovability.

Who knows, maybe someday we'll get married, but right now we feel good about the life we are trying to create. We feel secure in the commitment we each bring to growing and learning together, even if that means together *right now*, not together *forever*.

CHAPTER 1

Finally, Someone with Tools. Oh Fuck!

Vanessa

I've only had a handful of "knowings." An immediate deep sense in my body and my soul that I am on the right path or that something is truly *meant*. One of those knowings was that John and I would be together. When people ask how we met, I still very assuredly reply, "I manifested him." What I realize now is that my "knowings" don't always include all of the important information . . . like if things will be easy, or feel good, or how long they will last.

One of my best friends turned me on to John's Instagram account months before I actually met him. She had been following him for some time and resonated with a lot of what he was talking about on his platform. He came up occasionally in my feed, but to be completely honest, I never paused much other than to like something or reshare it if it spoke to me.

However, for some reason, on one particular day, after reading one particular post of his, I stopped and went deeper. I wish I could remember what the post actually said, but it caused me to go to John's page and start scrolling through it. I clicked through images and quotes. Read a few of his blogs, listened to him speak in a few videos.

I felt something. It's hard to pinpoint exactly what it was that John stirred in me at that moment, or why. I was coming out the other side of a bout of depression after a breakup that really shook me to my core. It was the first time I had experienced depression. I had known sadness and grief, longing and regret, but whenever others, even clients, had described depression, I hadn't been able to truly feel into what they meant. But the few months leading up to this rediscovery of John's Instagram page had been rough. Not getting off the couch or wanting to see anyone. Barely eating or working out. I was in the throes of a massive reconciliation of what it meant to continually date in a state of projection. Meaning, dating someone because of who they "could be," choosing not to see red flags because it didn't fit into the narrative of them or us that I had constructed in my head, or falling in love with who I *thought* they were and not seeing them for the messy and complicated human being they *actually* were. I had clawed my way through the past few months and was finally in a place of recognizing my pattern and committing to changing it.

Projection: Placing outside of ourselves and onto others the components of ourselves that we are incapable of seeing, whether because they are unconscious or because we find them unacceptable or shameful.

I shared John's post with that same best friend via direct message. My message to her read: "I find this guy to be incredibly attractive. From what I can tell he's single, lives in LA, and we have a mutual friend. I'm going to date him." Her response: "Ha! Yea ok. He has like 70k followers. You're going to date him huh?" To which I replied, "Yup."

A major synchronistic detail that possibly fueled my confidence was that I already had time on my calendar to go hiking with our mutual friend, Jason, so I decided to ask him about John. As Jason and I were hiking and talking about my recent move to LA and my career transition, my intention was to bring John up to him and ask him to pass along my number. But before I ever got the chance to say anything, Jason looked at me and said, "I have this friend that I feel like you would really get along with. He's on IG as The Angry Therapist."

I played it cool. "Oh? I don't think I know him." For the next twenty minutes Jason described him to me. Before I agreed that he could pass along my number, I did have one thing I needed to know for sure: "Does he date white girls?" An odd question, I know, but my recent breakup that had left me heartbroken and struggling to get off the couch was with a man who told me five months into dating pretty seriously that he didn't see a future with me because I was white. And while I respected and understood his connection to his culture, I was still healing from that experience and didn't want to get hurt again in the same way. Jason said he would check with John and give him my number in the meantime.

That night John texted. I was sitting on my yoga mat, about to go into class. My heart skipped. It was really crazy to me how this whole thing was going down. I have always been known as someone who "makes things happen." Once I set my mind on something, it usually becomes mine if only because of my focus and determination, but this felt bigger than my tenacity. This felt like something larger was at play that I couldn't see or understand.

We bantered a bit, and then he set up a "real" date. Dinner reservations on a Sunday evening. No coffee, no "let's go grab a drink." A real date, from the jump. I was impressed.

It was abundantly clear from our very first date that John possessed something that I had never found in another man. I had dated men who were self-aware (-ish), men who meditated and took care of themselves, men who talked the talk. But John looked at me in a way that disarmed me. He looked at me like he was really listening. Like he was invested in understanding this dynamic, digging deeper, exploring if this was something more than just attraction. Like he was just as interested in breaking old patterns and changing how he participated in relationships as I was.

We were both therapists with a hunger for dissecting relationships and the human experience, and that gave us a connection that I hadn't experienced with anyone before. When we talked, we dipped so swiftly below our outer layers and into our core selves that I could have stayed in that depth of connection forever.

I'd like to say that from that point forward it was a storybook romance, but it wasn't. It was the hardest first few months of a relationship I've ever had. I don't think we had a "honeymoon phase," because John spent most of that time doubting the relationship, and I spent most of it trying to decide if this was worth fighting for.

Four months in, he asked me to come with him on a semi-work trip to Costa Rica. He wanted to travel and spend time together. After going through a few cycles of doubting us and pulling away, leaving me feeling not chosen, John was finally choosing me by asking me to come with him on this trip, right? This invitation felt like maybe he was coming around and deciding he did really want me, want us. So I went, even with all of my doubts and insecurities still fully present. And then *bam*. The same pattern of appearing to choose me and then changing his mind happened again. Right in the middle of the trip, he emotionally bailed. He got weird, he pulled inside, and he couldn't have made it more obvious that he did not want me or want to be with or around me. I hit my emotional breaking point. I broke down as he talked to me about his "not knowing" about us. It was the first time I had cried in front of him, and I remember very clearly telling him through tears that we should break up.

I spent the following morning in a hammock overlooking the jungle treetops, dissecting the situation on

WhatsApp with two of my friends, who were a world away from me. "Fuck him. I'm so over this shit. When we get back I'm done with this relationship, I'm done with him." I remember my friend who had initially connected me to John's IG expressing such disappointment that who he portrayed himself to be was not who he really seemed to be. "I cannot believe he got you all the way out there where you're completely isolated and then dropped this bomb. Fuck him." After some more "fuck hims" were exchanged and agreed upon and the tears were wiped away, I breathed deeply and went to go shower. We still had four days left on the trip.

And in those four days I did what I always do: I compartmentalized it all and put a smile on my face to make sure no one felt like they needed to take care of me or would even notice that I was hurting. We finished the trip without any more apparent conflict.

It was on that trip that all of my projections started dissolving in front of my eyes in real time. I was struck with the intense realization that perhaps I had put John on a pedestal because he was a therapist who wrote about himself and relationships in a deep way. He talked like he knew things. But what was he showing me in real life? He was just another guy who had intimacy issues and hadn't worked through his bullshit. Another guy who said one thing but did another. Another guy who talked a big game about the work he had done, but who hid behind his past and his fear when it came time to put it into practice. He made me feel like he didn't want me. As I tried to convince him that he did, I had already convinced myself that being with someone like him was the answer.

During that Costa Rica trip I realized that I was furious with John, but also embarrassed—for assuming this time would be different just because he was a therapist.

John

Jason ran up to me and asked, "Do you date white girls?" I felt insulted. The question seemed racist. But I know he didn't mean it that way. Besides, we were at the gym, where there's that layer of locker-room verbiage. Verbal chest bumps. Machismo. I replied, "I date all girls." He then said he had a therapist for me. I was insulted again. I told him I didn't just date therapists. *What's wrong with you?* I thought. But I was secretly touched that Jason thought of me.

I hadn't been on a date in a while because I was being "single on purpose," which is a practice I had come up with for growing and investing in Self while free and alone. I came up with the idea because I had a horrible pattern of getting into long-term relationships too fast. I would meet someone. There would be a connection. The next thing I knew we were having breakfast for dinner, walking on egg-shells, and splitting the rent. So even though I was touched that Jason thought of me for his white girl therapist friend, I told myself, *John, you will not get into another long-term relationship.*

Instead, I had vowed to only date and do things that made me feel insecure and bad about myself. I was tired of commitment. I wanted to experience debauchery. Wake up next to someone I didn't like. Have sex on drugs. You get the idea.

Maybe you need a bit more context. When I was in my twenties and thirties, I was in a relationship that ended in marriage and then *really* ended in divorce. That relationship took up my headspace through many of my younger years, and I always suspected that I missed out on certain experiences. It might sound bizarre, but I now intended to have those experiences many of my clients were trying to undo. I wanted to know what some of them felt like for myself.

But none of that happened, save some sprinkled dating and one innocent night of Ecstasy and conversation with someone I had met online a while ago and finally got around to meeting in person. It felt more like two high school kids under the bleachers than a wild one-night stand. It was nice, and that was that. Things never play out as you imagine.

Enter Vanessa. Jason gave me her number and her social handles. After scrolling through her entire Instagram feed (all the way to her very first post, which everyone pretends like they don't do), I asked her out on a date at a restaurant right next door to my apartment. I could literally throw a quarter and hit it. It wasn't me being lazy. It was one of my favs and on her list to try.

As far as dates go, I was pleasantly surprised. We accidentally took home each other's leftovers, which was the hook to another meeting. But I was confused, because my brain didn't know where to file this. I knew I didn't want a relationship. I wasn't done being single on purpose. But she was. Then she touched me. Literally. Her touch felt *different*. I know that sounds hokey, but it's true. Yes, she studied Reiki, so maybe that had something to do with it. But her touch had a comfort and calm to it that I hadn't felt before. It felt greater than both of us. And it lingered. Making me more confused. And this confusion would set the relationship up for failure. Actually it wasn't the confusion. It was me denying it instead of really looking at it. Turning my cheek to my truth and just going with it because it felt good and made sense. That's where I was irresponsible.

Unlike Vanessa, I didn't let out a sigh of relief because she was a therapist. It was the complete opposite for me. Instead, I held my breath. I could finally be exposed here. No more being the "expert" in the relationship. Now someone could call me out on my shit instead of assuming it was her fault just because I had letters after my name. No more hiding behind theories, concepts, and 10,000-plus hours of helping people with *their* relationships. Vanessa was my kryptonite. I had met my match. And I was terrified.

I paid sixty grand with interest for EQ. I worked really hard for these emotional tools. And subconsciously, I felt I needed them to make up for anything I was lacking on the outside. I used my therapist knowledge base as armor against my insecurities. I had finally turned my bib into a cape, a cape I wore proudly in my relationships. Relationships and personal development was *my* major. Never theirs. This made it easy to deflect, hide, not take ownership, and move conversations back toward the other person at every turn, like we were trained to do with our clients.

But my expertise also prevented me from doing work on myself. Behind The Angry Therapist there was still an unhealthy, reactive, jealous, controlling, defensive boy. Vanessa would be the first to discover him.

Vanessa

Even though we finished off the Costa Rica trip at a small, romantic hotel with some good food and hot sex, I wasn't fully present. I had so much brewing inside me that would carry over into the next few weeks of our relationship. When we got back to Los Angeles, I made a decision. I was going to break relationship patterns that no longer served me.

I was no longer going to base my self-worth on whether or not the other person in the relationship, romantic or otherwise, was choosing me. I had spent my life contorting who I really was in order to be chosen. Telling myself, don't rock the boat. Say the right thing. Don't say the wrong thing. Be the cool girl who's not too needy. Don't have any needs, period. Be sexual, make them want you, but not so sexual that they only want that. Be funny, but don't talk too much. Don't be too much. Always be on. Like what they like. Give, give, give, but don't take. I was exhausted.

I decided during that trip that it didn't matter who chose me if I didn't choose me. I wanted to be able to be myself, fully authentic, in this relationship and in any relationships moving forward. But that was entirely on me. Maybe my "knowing" with John wasn't about him being my person. Maybe it was about the importance of him coming into my life so I could finally face myself and decide I was worth choosing.

I had spent years in therapy learning to trust myself, learning to hear what my gut, my intuition, was actually saying. I had finally listened to it when I left my last relationship. My gut had been telling me for years that this wasn't right for either of us and it was time to let go, and yet I had stayed and fought and forced it until a massive blowup ending was the only way out. At the time I thought I had finally learned the lesson. "I choose me" was what I told myself as I packed my bags and moved across the country alone, leaving everything I knew and everyone I loved behind. But since I had landed in LA, I had already had two relationships in which I was back in my old pattern of tap dancing and performing in order to be chosen. Now here was John, giving me the greatest gift— the opportunity to walk the walk.

So a couple days after we got back from Costa Rica I told him I needed time to think. I asked for a week without any contact. No texting, calling, or seeing each other. In that week I got clear: this wasn't about him, this was about me. Yes, I had fallen for John already, and my inner voice, based on my story, was screaming to do anything to keep him, to make him stay and not "abandon" me. But instead of listening to that voice, at the end of that week I let my gut do the talking.

I invited him over to talk. He showed up with flowers. I laid it out. "I can't do this anymore. This hot and cold. One minute you want me, and the next minute you pull the rug out from under me and I don't know which way is up. You're cold, you're in your head, you're disconnected. It makes me feel unsafe, like I can't trust you or me. I don't expect you to know that you want to be with me forever. I don't even know if I want to be with you forever, but you're either in or you're out. You either want to do this, to see where this goes, to see if there is something here to build together, or you don't." Essentially I told him to "shit or get off the pot."

His first response was "I thought you were calling me over here tonight to break up with me." Then he said, "I'm sorry I've made you feel unsafe. This is my stuff, not yours. I'm in."

Questions to Ask Yourself

Where in your life are you acting, performing, or phoning it in, in order to be chosen? What does that look like in your behavior? Are you open and honest with yourself and others, regardless of the possibility that they might not like it or could walk away? What does it feel like in your body in those moments when you don't show up authentically? When you stuff the real you down? Do you remember a moment when you did choose yourself? Do you remember how that felt?

The Practice

Sure, there can be big moments when we decide to choose ourselves. And these moments can feel amazing, empowering even. But listening to our knowings, hearing what our gut is saying in the everyday, the mundane, is a life-long practice. Pay close attention to the time when you choose to say or not say something in order to not rock the boat. Notice when you swallow asking for something, or when you shy away from having a hard conversation, or when the narrative in your head says something like "It's not worth it" or "What's the point?"

All the small moments like these that come up in a relationship are opportunities to choose yourself. In that one moment when you notice your fear but you say the thing anyway, you are turning up the volume on your intuition ever so slightly. You are telling yourself that you are worth choosing. It's in those micro moments that your sense of worth and value as a person will start to grow and strengthen. Think of each of those moments as a building block. Every time one of those blocks is laid, a foundation of Self is built.

CHAPTER 2

Happily Ever After Is Bullshit

We all grew up watching Disney movies and rom-coms, putting our hand over our heart and pledging that we would wait for our person to show up and hold us like they lost and then found us. We have been conned into believing in "the one," the one perfect person on this planet who we're supposed to spend the rest of our life with and who will probably be arriving on a white horse. Or in a Prius. Either way, once we find this person, everything will fall into place. We will finally be happy, complete, and living in peace and harmony in a castle, a blue lagoon, or a two-story Craftsman with matching BMWs and 2.2 beautiful kids.

The truth is, at some point in our thirties each of us woke

up and realized that happily ever after was bullshit and re-lationships take a fuck ton of work. We're not alone in that revelation, or in thinking that most adults eventually adopt the theory that "the one" is a fantasy and there are many *many* different people we could end up in healthy, happy, wonderful relationships with over the course of our lives.

But most of our clients have to be told explicitly to let go of the idea of "the one" when we start working together. Many of them couldn't get to this revelation on their own. In fact, holding so tightly to the security blanket idea of "the one" stripped them of the chance to even do the work in their relationships, because it gave them an escape hatch whenever they felt any sort of discomfort.

Does this sound familiar? Instead of working on yourself and your relationship, has this baked-in belief that there is a perfect person for you ever convinced you that you may be with the wrong person and the only solution is to dip? The idea of "the one" is a sickness that can act as a black light instead of a bridge. So, instead of building a healthy, sustain-able relationship that bridges differences and incompatibili-ties, we nitpick, get frustrated, feel entitled to our Prince or Princess Charming, and wonder who else is out there and if he or she will be coming to save us. Or complete us.

Ambivalence prevents us from truly learning about love. From shattering old blueprints, looking inward, and evolv-ing. It keeps us with one foot in the relationship and one foot out, creating distrust and unsafety—one of the most damaging dynamics in a relationship.

We're not talking here about the kind of ambivalence you have when you learn she has bad taste in movies. Or when you're deciding if his semi-strange fetish of biting your big toe while making love will be something you can pretend to like until you feel safe enough to say it's not really your jam. We're referring to everything on the other side of "I love you." When you guys are past the breakers (more on this in part 2!), after the two of you have mistakenly put each other's night guards on, when you have had that conversation with yourself that this time is going to be different. If you continue to be hot and cold at this point, if you are still using words or giving energy that is telling the other person you are unsure about all this (or even worse, words and energy that say different things), you are putting hairline cracks in the relationship. And over time the wall will come down. Or more accurately, a leg. A relationship with three legs, like a table, will always tip over. It's just a matter of time. This is not something we learned in therapy school or through helping thousands of clients with their relationships. It's something we learned personally in our own relationships and continue to work on in our current one.

John

"I'm going to get you some ice cream. Then get behind you later."

I hoped, with fingers crossed, that Vanessa would say something dirty or kinky back, something to remind me that there was still some hot-blooded energy running through our relationship.

However, in typical Vanessa fashion, she said: "If you get me ice cream, you're *definitely* not getting behind me tonight." Logical. Dairy *does* give her diarrhea. If she wanted to get technical, they did have vegan ice cream there. But that wasn't the point. She went left instead of right, again.

I wanted her to go with it. Give me some sort of flirtatious banter. Hit the ball back. But her response didn't match what I wanted. It highlighted our differences again, which brought me back to the beginning, reminding me that we didn't think the same, flirt the same, love the same.

And that meant she wasn't the right person. Right?

Even therapists who study this stuff for a living get it wrong. Here we were, months after getting back together in the wake of my ambivalence and doubt in Costa Rica. Finally committed to doing it differently this time. And yet, after the ice cream comment, I went cold. Something shifted in me from being curious about finding a flirtatious dynamic with Vanessa to doubting we would ever find it. For the rest of the day I was there, but not really. I drifted. I checked out. And in that moment, my ambivalence put a hairline crack in her ability to trust me. Again.

It really doesn't matter what form ambivalence takes. And it doesn't have to be obvious to be damaging. Because the obvious is obvious. It's the subtle moments in the day-to-day, the things you're not aware of, so you don't know the damage it does. Like when I pulled back and checked out after the ice cream incident. It was only for a few hours, but the energy was felt. Moments like this become paper cuts in a relationship. Eventually they start to produce blood. For example, subtle ambivalence can take the form of making plans you don't follow through on; not responding when your partner asks you something; bringing lukewarm energy to your conversations; not asking about your partner's day or how their yoga class was; not being part of making plans; forgetting to do things they asked you to do; making yourself eggs without asking if they would like some too; slipping out the door without saying goodbye—the list goes on.

The message I had been giving Vanessa with my moments of ambivalence was "I do not choose you." I didn't know it at the time, but that's what I was saying with my hot and cold. No, that wasn't my intention. I thought that, by being in this relationship, I was by default choosing her. But choosing someone is a daily, moment-to-moment action. It's not a onetime decision. Every time I felt and expressed ambivalence, the message I was giving Vanessa was "I do not choose you." And because this was the subtext, what was happening underneath, it was triggering for her.

In our experience, ambivalence is an epidemic in modern relationships and a key issue to tackle early on during the collision, lest it haunt the relationship down the line.

Now let's go deeper. Where was my ambivalence really coming from? Because it wasn't just about Vanessa not flirting with me the way I wanted her to. It went deeper than sex drives, which side of the brain I pull from, logical versus emotional, and expectations. My ambivalence mostly came from this warped idea of "the one." From a young age, just like you, I had been programmed to find "the one." Advertising, rom-coms, my parents, locker rooms—all told me that when I grew up I had to find "the one." That I would know who to spend the rest of my life with when I walked into a room, our eyes locked, and I felt it in the pit of my stomach that this was "the one."

Well, I thought I'd found that person. The relationship ended in divorce. But instead of abandoning the idea altogether, I felt the vise tightening, the pressure compounding. That person hadn't been "the one," so my "one" must still be out there. So I kept looking, and when I found someone I was interested in, but then things didn't line up the way I expected them to, the pressure of wondering if this person was "the one" shone an unfair black light on the relationship and caused me to second-guess, control, and ultimately drift. The idea of "the one" suffocated our love like a glass jar set over a lit candle. It didn't allow new love to grow. That wouldn't happen until I finally became aware of the problem with the idea of "the one."

The sad part is, I see the impact that ambivalence has on my clients' relationships all the time, so I should have known not to bring that energy into my own relationship. The hurt inflicted on a partner when you are ambivalent is extremely detrimental. My ambivalence came from putting expectations on Vanessa to be a certain way, act a certain way, love a certain way, because if she fit in that box—created by society, advertising, locker rooms, and my other love experiences— then she would be "the one." And I would no longer be searching. The experience she was having, though, as I put my expectations on her was one of feeling I was "hot and cold" or distant for no reason, unresponsive, disinterested, withholding, dismissive. Of feeling I was not choosing her.

Once I realized that all my ambivalence stemmed from the idea of "the one" and the message I was giving Vanessa ("I don't choose you"), I was able to drown my ambivalence.

How? I smashed the box, tossed the checklist, and threw away the expectations. Or at least, I did that the best I could. It didn't happen overnight, and I still struggle with it today. But knowing where something comes from takes away its power. You're now in the trailer watching the makeup artist turn the actor into a monster. The curtain is pulled back and the lie is exposed. Truth is revealed.

When I was able to see this, something transformative happened. I started to find beauty in the contrast. I found things I liked about Vanessa that I'd dismissed before, that I didn't allow myself to see because my only lens was comparison—the monster. A new person emerged, one not controlled or tainted by my past and my "shoulds." And for me what emerged was growth. Also, realizing that my ambivalent behavior made her feel unchosen allowed me to stretch my empathy. Because I have felt unchosen before. I felt unchosen and alone toward the end of my marriage. And no one should feel that way. It's one of the worst feelings in this world. It's better to put that love out of its misery so it doesn't suffer.

Vanessa

Unlike John, I never grew up believing in "the one." Even though I watched all the same movies, I had a mother who was frequently single and fiercely independent. She instilled in me the idea that I didn't need anyone. It morphed for me into a belief that relying on others leads to disappointment. Better to just follow the thrill and enjoy it while it lasts, because it will probably end. Reflecting back as an adult, I realize this attitude came from her own broken heart over the person she thought was "the one" early on in her life. She never fully recovered from that heartbreak, and I think the rest of her relationships suffered because of it—and my relationships may have suffered in kind.

The funny thing is, although I didn't believe in the fairy-tale version of "the one" that was shown to me, the idea of a Prince Charming, I do have my own warped thinking because of that early programming. In my mind, and through my upbringing, "the one" wasn't a knight on a white horse. He was just the person who would accept me no matter what. "The one" was someone you never had conflict with. Who you could say anything to, do whatever you wanted, no matter how hurtful, and they would stay and love you anyway. Sounds perfect, right?

Well, if perfect acceptance and bliss had to be the norm, then conflict, discomfort, and being held accountable in a relationship meant that you couldn't possibly be right for each other. So you can imagine how hard it has been to sustain a relationship. Or rather, to sustain a relationship while being honest and true to myself. I spent most of my relationships doing cartwheels to keep them as conflict-free as possible, all at the expense of my voice, my needs, and being seen and accepted for who I really was. Those cartwheels looked a lot like people-pleasing, carrying a shitload of resentment, and shutting down when there was conflict, until the rift became so big, there was no way to repair it. How could a relationship that had no foundation of honest communication, healthy fighting, respect, and open expression of needs and hurts have a chance of being repaired? It wasn't stable to begin with.

John is no different from the others. Or at least in the beginning he wasn't. There has been a pretty constant tug-of-war feeling in my relationship with John—between him being present and feeling like he is committed to "us" and him pulling away and very obviously doubting it all. When I respond to him in a way that doesn't fit the narrative he has in his head, he tends to use the term "disconnect"—there's a disconnect between us. Our love languages are different. His way of flirting is very verbal (and sexual), while I communicate through touch, humor, and doing things for him. The "disconnect" leads him to feel like I don't flirt with him, I don't find him sexy, I'm not interested in him. The disconnect leads me to feel like what I *am* doing isn't enough for him, to get frustrated by what feels like more expectations on my plate. And just like that, in zero to sixty, the disconnect usually leads him to pull inward, go cold, and retreat into his head. He pulls away and gives me ambivalence, and I'm left feeling unsafe. Not a good place for someone whose story is "there is conflict, he doesn't get me or accept me, we should be in sync all of the time."

Let's pause here and ask a preliminary question before we get to the more robust "Questions to Ask Yourself" section. Ask yourself if you find yourself doubting your partner's intentions, or even your relationship, when there is conflict or a glaring difference between you.

Yes, the idea of "the one" being the person who accepts you no matter what does sound pretty great initially, but does it sound realistic? To be in sync all the time means to be sacrificing a part of yourself for your partner's sake, or allowing your partner to sacrifice their true self for your sake. Believe me, if you are in perfect sync at every moment, someone isn't being their true self. Being perfectly in sync also closes off your ability to grow and evolve, both as an individual and as a couple. We evolve when we're able to accept differences, to see someone for who they truly are, not who we wish they were, and also when we're able to be honest about ourselves with the other person and have them also love and accept us for who we are.

Something important to note here: I'm not talking about major differences. Religious beliefs, politics, wanting or not wanting kids, values, life priorities, etc., etc., etc., can all be reason enough that a relationship can't or shouldn't continue. The non-negotiables are different for all of us, and something we should really know and understand about ourselves. With many of my clients, I've done an exercise—and done it myself—called "Non-Negotiables versus Preferences." You will do this exercise soon, in chapter 4.

One of the best ways to "sync up" with your partner is to accept that sometimes being in sync is being out of sync. When I respond to John's verbal flirtation with my own form of humor, even though it doesn't end with both of us feeling in perfect harmonious bliss, isn't there something to celebrate when two people who love each other are being themselves? At first glance, John might feel otherwise, but if he knows I'm responding in the way that he prefers only for his sake, a way that feels fake or forced for me, that's an immediate turnoff for him. It becomes part of our work in the relationship to then sit with the disappointment around us not being in sync, and then to see each other for who and what we truly are and give each other credit for the ability to show up authentically in that moment.

Sometimes it feels like John and I are missing each other, and sometimes it feels like we are in lockstep. I haven't quite figured out the formula yet to keep us in lockstep all the time. But I'm also beginning to realize that's just it. There is no formula. We are different people, with different ways of flirting and with different love languages. We are never going to be in sync all the time, and it's silly of me (either of us really, but I'll stick to "I" statements here) to expect otherwise. For me, the growth is in this realization that these differences don't make us incompatible. They make us two different people, and with our different needs, we have to speak up and ask for what we want or risk being disappointed and hurt, a lot.

In spite of our differences, we chose this relationship be-cause we knew . . . wait, maybe I should continue speaking only for myself . . . I chose this relationship because I knew, even though we had a lot of differences, our similarities were ones that were fundamental to what I wanted in a long-term partnership. We are in sync in our shared goals, ambitions, and independent natures as well as in our ability to give each other all of the necessary space. We're both engaged and active parents, we're both supportive and kind to each other, we're both seekers with high expectations for self-reflection and continual growth, and we both want to build something honest no matter what. Plus, John is the silliest and kindest man I have ever dated. I tend to be a more serious person, sometimes a cynic. He reminds me to not take things so seriously.

So the question then is, isn't it okay to be out of sync sometimes but still be present to the reality of who I am and who my partner is as a multifaceted and complicated person?

Here is where our differences have landed us. John hits the ball to me in his own way, and I respond in my own way. John sometimes feels rejected, and I sometimes feel put upon. And then we talk it out, again, and come to the same conclusion—the stories that we are telling ourselves are not true.

Why? Because I never learned that conflict is part of a healthy relationship. I never learned that while everyone is flawed, our only responsibility is to own our flaws, apologize when we have hurt someone, and try to learn and grow from these conflicts and mistakes. I always thought that when I found "the one," we would laugh every day, I would never get triggered or be made to feel like I had to step it up a little, and I would be able to just relax, trust, and finally stop questioning everything all the time.

* * *

Our belief is that we have many "the ones" in our lifetime. Every person you have loved was "the one" at that time. "The one" is the person you consciously choose to love today. Not who you used to love, could love, or wish you could love. It's who you are choosing to love right now, as hard or easy as that is. Once you choose to stop loving that person, he or she is no longer "the one." It's that simple. A thriving, healthy, sustainable relationship is built on more than goose bumps. Notice how all Disney movies end at the wedding? You don't ever get to see the part where five years into their marriage Cinderella is yelling at Prince Charming to just "pick up your dirty socks and put them in the damn hamper"—for the hundredth time that week. Ending the story at the wedding keeps us from seeing the messy human reality of long-lasting relationships and the real work they take.

Why is it important to look at it this way? First, let's boil down what love really is. **At the end of the day, love is a daily choice to be emotionally responsible to someone.** If you're not emotionally connected, it's not love. It may be lust or convenience or an arrangement or a way to avoid being alone, and if any of that works for you, that's fine, right? But it's not love.

If you don't think you're with "the one," or if you believe someone else "got away," you will not give the relationship you are in your all. Instead, you will dream, fantasize, scroll, and fill in a lot of blanks. You won't be present or grateful. You will doubt, set unrealistic expectations, chase something that isn't real, and maybe even sabotage.

Now the not so obvious. If you believe you're with "the one," that belief implies that you're supposed to be with this person. You guys were *intended*. Things were meant to line up this way. And if they don't, you're going to be confused or, worse, devastated. Why aren't things perfect and easy? Once the doubting and questioning creeps in, you can begin to drift emotionally, even if you don't mean to. And it can be a slow burn. It doesn't have to be overnight. But now you're elsewhere.

The thing about "hard" is, no one likes hard. We're not wired to like hard. Because hard means discomfort. Hard means breaking patterns, looking inward, taking ownership, doing things you're not used to. Hard means you could be wrong. Hard means it's no longer just about you. But hard is where substance and depth live. Not in easy. Easy feels good. It's sugar, highly addictive, and temporary. But most importantly, easy creates ceilings. Not just for you but also for the relationship. If you just want something that feels good, there will be no love journey for you, and without a journey, there will be no growth. Love is about depth, not width. Easy equals width, and believing in "the one" is easy.

Nothing of value in this world comes from easy.

Including love.

Questions to Ask Yourself

Do you believe in "the one"? If so, how has that belief affected your relationships, past or present? Have you been the one who's hot and cold in a relationship? What feeling has ambivalence created in you? Where does it come from? Have you ever spoken up and had an honest conversation around where your ambivalence is coming from? Or have you been on the receiving end of ambivalence? If so, have you ever spoken up about how their hot and cold makes you feel? When in your past have you sacrificed yourself, your authenticity, to avoid conflict or to avoid facing a difference?

The Practice

Hold yourself or your partner accountable when you or they "check out."

If it's you, see if you can pinpoint what happens right before you feel like retreating. What was said? What emotions came up? Put words to it: "I realize that when we talk about X, I get really uncomfortable because of X and I pull away. That isn't fair and I'm going to work on it." Then ask yourself what working on it will look like. This is the most important piece, and it's where most people drop the ball.

If it's your partner who retreats, speak up when you feel the energy shift. Tell your partner how it makes you feel. "When I feel you pull away, it makes me feel really unsafe, like you are not invested in the relationship, or like you are judging me as a person."

Remember, by practicing speaking up and being honest, you aren't asking yourself or your partner to commit to more than either of you is ready for. You are simply asking for honest communication about where you are in the relationship. This gives all parties an opportunity to be on the same page and to make informed decisions about how and what they want to invest in the relationship, and what they want the relationship to feel like.

There are always two people in a relationship. It can't be one person being all in and committed to making things work while the other is phoning it in or disappearing every time they get uncomfortable. So ask yourself if you are doing more or less than your 50 percent. What would it look, sound, and feel like to even out the relationship workload?

CHAPTER 3

The Lightning in a Bottle Is Actually Dysfunction

Be mindful of people who feel like home, when home wasn't a safe place to be.

—@THEMINDGEEK

Sometimes I think people are using the term [trauma bond] to pathologize an intense feeling in order to avoid vulnerability.

—MC MCDONALD

John

After the Costa Rica trip, it was smooth sailing for a while. Nothing but calm waters and clear blue skies. I was in it, and Vanessa started to feel safe, maybe for the first time since we started dating. Then out of nowhere I found myself shutting down again. It was like a possession. A spirit taking over my body, without warning. I snapped back like a rubber band, panicking and questioning everything. *Am I with the right person? Do I want to spend the rest of my life with her? Can this work if we speak different love languages? She's a vegan and I like meat. What if she never scratches my back hard enough?* You know, all the questions we don't have answers to but try to answer anyway, which pulls us out of the relationship and into our spinning head. Something I tell my clients to not do. Easier said than done.

The thing about "doing the work," as they say in our field, is that sometimes you take one step forward and two back. Growth is not a straight, consistent line. It's long and squiggly and unpredictable. I don't know why I lost traction. Maybe because things were good and that meant we were getting closer to the island. I started to see the outline of a picket fence.

I knew I wanted to eventually be in another committed relationship. But was this the one I wanted to be in? Everything made sense on paper. Vanessa was smart and beautiful and had emotional intelligence and a really nice butt. What more could I ask for? But there was this powerful resistance, and I couldn't understand it. And if you know me, you know it's impossible for me to hide things.

I took the question to my therapist.

Therapist: Are you sure it's not because you need to sow your oats? You said you were on a path of debauchery before you guys met. But you didn't get far.

John: I don't know. Maybe that's a part of it. But there's something else. That lightning isn't there.

Therapist: Explain that. What do you mean by "lightning"?

John: I remember when I first met my ex-wife I saw halos and shit. There was this crazy draw that felt undeniable. I wanted to lose myself in her.

Therapist (*after a pause*): Which you actually did. (*Silence as John thinks about this.*)

Therapist: If you compare both relationship dynamics, what's missing in this one that was in that one?

John: That crazy draw, like me wanting to capture her. The chase. Not in a playing games kind of way. It's animalistic. Like I want to control her or something.

Therapist: So maybe Vanessa isn't controllable and that's confusing to you? And because of this, and comparing it to your other relationship when you were much younger, you think it's lacking chemistry. But you also said the relationship with your ex-wife was dysfunctional. Neither of you had done any work to better yourselves. I wonder if you would still see "halos" if you were to meet your ex, after she had done some work on herself, for the first time today? Simply put, maybe the lightning you felt with your ex-wife, which you seem to compare all your relationships to, was actually dysfunction.

John: And since Vanessa has worked on herself, that dysfunction is not there, so my body is telling me maybe this isn't the one?

Therapist: Sometimes chemistry isn't what we think it is. *(This hits John hard.)*

Therapist: And you know as well as I do that it takes much more than a "halo" to build a healthy, sustainable relationship.

WHAT IS ATTRACTION?

When we think about attraction, we think about nice butts (or maybe that's just me?) and strong arms, piercing eyes, intelligence, banter, humor, similar tastes in books and films, and maybe tacos as a shared love language. However, attraction also has an unexplainable undercurrent that no one talks about and that is more powerful than all of the above combined. Let's call it "the sticky"—the dysfunction between two people that gets mistaken for chemistry. The familiar smell from the rocky and chaotic upbringing we're unconsciously trying to trace. The residue from our stories.

There are many other terms for this feeling: "lightning in a bottle," "love at first sight," "meant to be." We have found through working with clients that "I don't know what it is but there's something about him," or "When you know, you know," may sometimes be perfectly good explanations for that feeling that draws you to another person . . . but it also may be coming from an unhealthy place. We're often blind to that possibility because we've been programmed by movies and romance novels and our best friends telling us that what we feel is rare and special and we should just let ourselves fall back willingly with our arms folded and eyes closed. But it's a feeling worth examining because it can actually be a red flag.

What most people don't consider is that the sticky can be coming from what Freud termed "repetition compulsion," or what's also called "compulsion to repeat." In psychoanalytic theory, repetition compulsion is an unconscious need to reenact early traumas in an attempt to overcome or master them. Such traumas are repeated in a new situation symbolic of the repressed prototype. Repetition compulsion compels us to resist therapeutic change, since the goal of therapy is not to repeat but to remember the trauma and to see its relation to present behavior.

Repetition compulsion: Either actively or passively (unconsciously) repeating a behavior pattern from an emotional or physical experience in an attempt to master, make sense of, and integrate it, or until the "lesson" is learned.

When we go through an experience that we can't grasp or make sense of, we are compelled to repeat it over and over so that we can try to better understand it. We may unconsciously re-create the feelings we had in childhood that we equate with love. The behavior we keep repeating can be based on an unhealthy narrative we have around our worth or deservingness. In extreme cases the behavior pattern can even derive from what has been dubbed a "trauma bond": an intense emotional attachment seen exclusively in situations of abuse.

*   *   *

Take two people.

A girl who had something taken away from her as a child. Maybe her voice or her self-esteem. At home, her parents were always screaming. Or worse, were silent. Maybe she had to be an adult when she wasn't one yet. Mom was too busy numbing herself with television or white wine. Dad seemed "perfect," except for his iron fist. Or maybe there was no dad, only boyfriends who came and went with the seasons. This little girl spent a lot of time alone, outside playing with boys, some of whom were aggressive, with no supervision or boundaries. She accepted this as the norm, as "boys will be boys." When she allowed them into her emotional space, the resulting predator-prey dynamic laid the tracks for abusive and toxic relationships when she got older. But as a child, she was willing to accept anything in exchange for approval, love, and acceptance. And seeking acceptance led her into situations of unwanted advances and experimentation. She turned inward, locked her emotions in a box, blamed herself for her dysfunctional family, and found home in the boys with no boundaries. Something was taken from her. Her safe space. Her voice. Her innocence. Her childhood. This is your prey.

Then you have a boy. There was addiction in his family tree. Maybe not for him or his parents, but for his grandparents, or even further up the gene tree. Wherever it started, the addict was an adult child, with low emotional intelligence and surrounded by enablers. Drug of choice? Sex, gambling, alcohol, food, anything to numb, escape, or feel something good for once. It didn't matter. Biology and the multigenerational transmission process allowed the addiction to be passed down from branch to branch of the family tree. On a budding leaf way down by the trunk sat our boy, alone, angry, confused, and ready to pay it forward. He was reactive, impulsive, and aggressive. Behaviors developed from not having a stable and safe home life. So he grew up impatient and impulsive, with low self-control. Now he has a venti size ego and no concept of rules or consequences. He is defensive and ignores you and abuses you and makes you feel like it's you, not him. This is your predator, what we might call a "bad boy."

This man will smell familiar to the woman who grew up around boys with no boundaries. That's why she gravitates toward him. He will break her heart and become a raging addict. And whether he admits it or not, she matters to him, and that terrifies the shit out of him. He's afraid of losing her or really showing her his true self. Because that would require looking at himself and his shortcomings. He would have to run toward himself, not away, something he's never learned how to do. Simply put, he doesn't have the tools to love anyone in a healthy way, especially himself. She sees his heart, and it's big. But his reactions and unhealthy ways of coping are bigger.

> **Multigenerational transmission process:** The process by which, through conscious teaching or unconscious programming, the older generation passes down to the younger generation their ways of handling emotions and stress, behaviors, and ways of relating to others. Transmission that remains unconscious will cycle through the generations, continually passing down these "lessons."

Put the prey and predator in a room full of "normal" people at a party and see what happens. They will find each other by the end of the night. Their attraction is almost instinctive, animalistic, and definitely unconscious. It's that lightning we all search for, but can't always explain. Now we have the perfect ingredients for a deliciously dysfunctional relationship. Without healing, tools, and self-growth, the cycle repeats itself. Again. And again.

Predator-prey is just one type of relationship dynamic, and of course this description is overly simplified. Women can be predators just as men can be prey, and the dynamic can show up in same-sex relationships as well.

As therapists, Vanessa and I have heard a version of the story many many times. Just with different names. What's important is to help our clients become aware of what's running underneath. That "chemistry" may actually be residue from their stories, a "sticky" from their past. And because this person feels familiar, we can mistake that feeling for love and go chasing the high without seeing the cliff. Without this awareness, we can keep falling into the same unhealthy relationships, over and over again, with only the faces changing. This is why so many people say, "I keep falling for the same person."

Breaking this pattern starts with questioning the attraction. Where is it coming from? Is it true chemistry creating the powerful tug, or is it really a dysfunctional relationship dynamic that smells familiar? These are questions we not only had to help our clients answer. We also had to answer them ourselves.

Your soulmate is not someone who will come into your life peacefully. It will be the person who comes to make you question things, to change your reality. Someone who marks a before and after in your life. It will not be the idealized person you fantasized about, but an ordinary person who challenges you and makes you better.

Vanessa

When I met my college boyfriend, the one I called—or used to call—"my soulmate," I was instantly attracted to him. I wanted him. And I wanted him to want me. When we fell, we fell hard. I remember feeling physical pain in my body when he wasn't around me. Like I couldn't breathe. And then, when the relationship crumbled, I lay on the bathroom floor and cried for days. I lost weight. I couldn't get out of bed and barely completed my last semester of college. It was as if I had lost an appendage. In looking back over all of my other relationships, it's very obvious to me that I have never felt that way about anyone else. Not John, not anyone. As I moved into my midtwenties after that breakup, I began the hunt for that feeling again. Thinking that was what love felt like, and that anything less than that wasn't real.

So much with my college boyfriend lined up: our humor, our love for music, our passion and drive for bigger things. He let me take up space and didn't make me feel guilty for it. He let me mother him and take care of him without pushing back on it as nagging. He loved that I was loud and opinionated, that I "didn't take shit from anyone," and he actually leaned on me for help in that area. I felt seen, understood, and accepted in a way I had never felt until that point.

We also never fought. And I mean *never*. In the more than five years we were together, I can count on one hand the number of times we even argued, and those times were almost all in the last six months of the relationship. To me, this meant we were perfect for each other. *When it's right, you don't fight.* And the most important thing? The truest essence of lightning in a bottle to me? It was the thing I still struggle with: he *chose* me. He always chose me. Over all else. (At least until he didn't.)

Why am I going back in time and telling you the story of a past love? Because now, as an adult who has done a lot of relationship work and been through a few more rounds of relationship beginnings and endings, I know he represented parts of me that were unseen, unheard, and not accepted in my upbringing. He told me, without telling me, that men could be relied upon. That they could show up and choose you, love you, accept you, and not leave. That they could save you from yourself. That they could be a safe hiding place from the things you hated about yourself but didn't yet understand or want to understand.

He also, in the end, verified the exact narrative I had around men and around myself going into the relationship. That they actually *do* always leave. That I can't rely on them. That you have to show up in a certain way and be a certain person to keep them. That once it gets hard and rocky they bail. That "keeping him" ends up being your part to play in a relationship. The work-doer. The caretaker. The peacekeeper.

The next two relationships ran a similar course: they also *chose* me in the beginning. They made it very clear they *wanted* me. And because, growing up, so much of me didn't feel chosen or wanted in many ways, *that* to me was love. Being wanted equated to existing or mattering, and it meant they wouldn't leave. No conflict meant the relationship was right (even if there wasn't conflict only because I never spoke up or rocked the boat). None of the other stuff mattered.

And in both of those relationships, it felt like the more "me" I really was, the more work I did to discover and reconnect to them, to embrace and love them in all of the messy, imperfect ways they showed up, the less they "chose" me. That just further cemented the narrative I had that the only way to be chosen was to be someone else. Someone who they wanted, all of the time. I had such a fear of being left, of being abandoned, that I would have done or not done anything to keep them choosing me. It took me many years (and my collision with John) to see my own repetition compulsion for what it was: a need to prove to myself that my imperfect self could be loved and accepted by only going after men who chose me when I was playing a part. Unconscious patterns are a bitch, am I right?

Cut to John.

The fight we had on our Costa Rica trip was really just the tipping point around my need to feel chosen coming up against his relationship checklist in order for me to be "the one." The conflict for both of us wasn't with our relationship in the present, but with the ghosts of relationships past.

What does this look like for us today? For me, the feeling of not being chosen has continued to show up as a central point of conflict. Like John with his checklist, I have to remember the truth: *It's not logical, it's upbringing. It's wiring. It's patterning.*

YOU ARE YOUR OWN LIGHTNING

To me, feeling chosen equals lightning in the bottle. That feeling is the spark for me. It's the draw, the feeling I equate with love. And now, years into the relationship with John and after a few more cycles of ambivalence, my revelation is that you can't actually rely on other people to give you that "lightning in a bottle" feeling. Because when they do, there's usually more going on than meets the eye, something beneath the surface. A larger force at play is drawing you toward each other.

Patterns and programming are worth examining closely,

but most of us never do it, because that initial "lightning in a bottle" feeling is amazing. You feel invincible. Like a missing piece of you has been found and clicked into place. It's like how I imagine (and have heard addicts recount) heroin feels the first time you try it. A warmth that spreads over you, taking away all of your pain, worry, fear, and emptiness. And that feeling is why we get addicted to love. Why we equate the lightning in a bottle with love. And why (or at least partly why) over 50 percent of long-term monogamous relationships fail.

Of course you have to have chemistry—those moments when you feel so seen and understood, it's almost unnerving. Chemistry is important, but chemistry isn't "it." We are each responsible for understanding the unconscious drives at play when we "choose" a relationship. What is fueling that spark, that feeling of instant bonding?

Instant bonding isn't always unhealthy, by the way. Sometimes it comes from a place of deep understanding, of feeling truly like the yin to someone's yang. But even in those moments it's still important to try to understand what's happening beneath the surface. Because it's through that understanding that when there's conflict—which there will always be in a healthy relationship—you can see yourself and the part you are playing. It's through that understanding that you take ownership of what you bring to the table and what you are responsible for. Without that understanding, you will resort to a whole lot of finger-pointing, playing the victim, and repeating unhealthy patterns.

I still have to work hard at choosing myself. In understanding that choosing myself is my lightning in a bottle, my sticky, I know it's something I need to work to give myself. Through conscious and mostly small moments of choosing myself (such as recognizing that my needs are worthy of expressing and expressing them; or not shutting down and getting defensive when John is upset with me but trying my best to listen and understand his POV; or letting John be mad or upset and not trying to fix it or hold it for him), I am telling myself that I am worthy of being chosen. And the more I show myself that I am worthy of being chosen, the less I rely on others to choose me.

Questions to Ask Yourself

The point of this chapter's discussion isn't to make you doubt your relationship, or the things about it that you feel you can trust and lean into. If your partner makes you feel a certain way, you should be able to trust that. We don't mean to say that you *only* feel a connection because it's a trauma bond or some sort of wiring from your past. Sometimes attraction is just attraction, and we don't need to pathologize it. But the bottom line is this: There are always four people in every relationship, not two. There are our two conscious minds, and then there are our two unconscious minds. While we think we are calling most of the shots when it comes to our chosen relationships (which includes friendships), we aren't. Our unconscious is. It is always attempting to heal old wounds, correct past mistakes, and repair historical hurts. Our unconscious is drawn to people who feel familiar, regardless of safety or true compatibility. Our job is to attempt to be aware of our old patterns, our unconscious pulls, so that we show up in our relationship as present and conscious as we can be. For our sake and our partner's.

So ask yourself: What does your partner bring up in you when the relationship is at its *best*? Do you feel seen? Put on a pedestal? Respected? Understood? Supported? Safe to express yourself? What about when the relationship is at its *worst*? Do you feel emotionally abandoned? Do you feel belittled? Disrespected? Underappreciated?

Now ask yourself the same two questions about your relationships with your primary caretakers growing up. How did you feel when the relationships were great? Did you feel safe? Did you feel like you made them proud? Were you respected? Now flip it. What about when these relationships were not so great? Did you feel like a disappointment? Not good enough? Did you feel misunderstood?

Now compare the two lists. When things are flowing smoothly, what are the similarities between these relationships? And when they aren't? When you feel emotionally activated in your current relationship, are you feeling an especially strong connection between your childhood and the present? It's important that we understand our emotional priming during our upbringing because it can create blueprints for our adult relationships that, if left unexamined, will allow us to build a faulty foundation for our relationship that will almost inevitably crumble at the first sign of a tremor.

For bonus points, ask yourself these same questions about your closest friendships, work relationships, and any other chosen person who is in your inner circle.

The Practice

Once we understand the connection between our upbringing and our current relationship, or our ways of choosing
relationships, we can start to be more conscious in our
choices, because we can't unknow what we've come to
know. Feeling "triggered" is usually a good place to start. It
takes time to develop the ability to notice when you have
been triggered *before* you react, but if you can see that you
are feeling an emotional response to something, pause. Sit
in the feeling for a moment and allow yourself to just feel it,
deeply. Inspect it, turn it over, and look at it from all sides.
Where do you feel this response in your body? What does
the sensation feel like? Heat? Tightness in your throat? Diz-
ziness? What's the first reaction you have and want to express? Do you have an urge to get defensive? Do you want
to verbally punch back and make the other person hurt?
Do you have a desire to run? To go hide and be alone? Are
you on the verge of tears? Answering these questions will
uncover some important information.

> **Triggered:** An intense emotional response that, viewed objec-
> tively, may be disproportionate to or larger than the event that
> provoked it.

Once you have gotten familiar with the sensation and the
reaction you want to take in response to it, we start to follow the thread backward to the "why?" This practice can be

helpful to do with a therapist, or with someone you trust to be nonjudgmental and neutral. You want to start connecting this present moment that has triggered this response in you with when and where you felt a similar feeling in the past. You want to write down all of the times you can remember feeling this way, whether in past romantic or friend relationships or with a parent or a teacher or a coach. Starting to connect current reactions to past experiences is a huge step in understanding how the past controls your present and future. It allows you to slow down, breathe into the present moment you are in, and make a decision about how you will respond *this time*. Bonus points for communicating, in the moment, the emotion, sensations, and desired reaction to the person who triggered them.

This practice is less about behaving in certain ways and more about connecting dots and learning where behavior comes from. Practicing knowing the why equates to a better understanding of Self. The more you can do that, the more your behavior starts to change naturally.

Self versus self: Carl Jung defined the "Self" (capitalized) as "the totality of one's being." It is the sacred and whole center of the personality and is the unification of consciousness, unconsciousness, and the ego. It represents the Psyche as a whole, whereas "self" (lowercase) represents the ego. Think of the self as a smaller circle within the larger, all-encompassing circle that is the Self.

CHAPTER 4

Finding Beauty in the Contrast

The beginning of love is to let those we love be perfectly themselves, and not to twist them to fit our own image. Otherwise we love only the reflection of ourselves we find in them.

—THOMAS MERTON

FENDER BENDER

Drew literally collided into Marcus. She was checking her Bumble, believe it or not, and didn't realize the car ahead was stopped at a fresh red light. She was notorious for rearending people and braced herself for another furious driver who would claim a fake injury and sue her. But she was taken aback by Marcus, not only by his chiseled face and seafoam-green eyes, but by how kind and understanding he was. She admitted to him that she was checking messages on her dating app, mostly as a subtle way of letting him know that she was single. She told him she would pay for the damages, which turned out to be just a few scratches on his bumper. He said it wasn't necessary. She insisted they exchange information, but he wouldn't have it. Instead, he shot her a smile and vanished. And just like that, he was gone.

Until they collided again. This time in a virtual chat room called "No One Got Away!" (we kid you not). It was a live chat that John created about love and dating to promote his new book at the time, *Single. On Purpose.* Drew saw Marcus's tiny little profile pic and recognized him instantly. She clicked on it, found his Instagram, and stalked the shit out of him. Coming across him again, she felt, was a sign from the universe. She had been single for a while now after being in many toxic relationships, and she was ready to build something healthy with someone. And the fact that he was "Single. On Purpose." was a very good sign. It meant he was working on himself as well.

After a few flirtatious DMs, they met for a walk on the beach, which led to kissing in the parking lot and sex behind a dumpster. Well, they were in a Volvo. And the "dumpster" was actually a cargo container at a construction site. Anyway, Drew loved it. This encounter made her feel alive, like making out with her high school crush under the bleachers, which never happened because she was too busy studying and being a "good girl." Marcus admitted that he had found her attractive when she rear-ended him, but he was in a relationship at the time and also running super late to an Al-Anon meeting he happened to be running.

Drew and Marcus became a couple instantly. They wanted to take it slow, but they didn't. They moved in together. Got a dog. Even shared a Google calendar so they knew each other's schedules and could plan accordingly. In sessions, Drew would remind me (John) that this one was different. "He's not only GQ, he's EQ!" I wasn't a big fan of her humor. According to her, he was the perfect guy. He had the ability to hold a safe space as well as a job. So then why were they sitting in front of John for a couples therapy session? Because they were drifting as fast as they had collided.

They were different. In every way. She was messy. He was organized. She liked meat. He was vegan. She believed in God. He believed in aliens. Her love language was words of affirmation and touch. His was acts of service. She liked chips. He liked cookies. Nothing matched up, and they didn't realize how different they were until they moved in together. Drew booked a session with John because she was at her wit's end. She didn't know what to do. She loved everything about this relationship except how different they were. It was new and "weird."

After a few sessions, I realized how much in her head she was about this. Drew literally had a list she had made of all their differences, which she kept adding to weekly. It's no wonder that she was contemplating ending it. She was obsessing about what was "wrong" in the relationship instead of feeding what was right or healthy or good—how Marcus made her feel, his ability to create a safe space, be vulnerable, consistent, communicative, and, oh yeah, good in bed. Basically all the ingredients for building a solid, healthy relationship. And also all the things she hadn't had in previous relationships but had always wanted. She knew all this but couldn't stop obsessing about their differences, so that's all she saw. John wanted to shake Drew. Not just because, as a therapist, he knew how rare it was to find that kind of relationship soil, but also because it was something he had struggled with in his own relationship.

Drew eventually broke up with Marcus. They both stopped seeing John. Then, a year later, he received an email from Drew. She was going through another breakup, this time with someone who was like the male version of her. She said it was refreshing at first. Until she realized he had no tools. Of course that relationship didn't last, and Marcus was now the "one that got away."

John

She finds puns funny. I do not. She thinks David Bowie is hot. I think he was an innovative artist, but hot? Come on. He looks like a goblin. She is well read. I am not. She'll keep a gift card that has 23 cents on it. I will not. She'll take one tiny bite of a dessert and take the rest to go. That makes no sense to me. I do CrossFit. She does yoga. I like raw fish. The smell of seafood makes her heave. She follows instructions when building things. I use them to wipe my sweat. Her love language is acts of service. Mine is words of affirmation. These are just some of the differences between Vanessa and me.

Unlike Drew, I did not create a list of those differences, but I did obsess about them. And this kept me in my head instead of present in the relationship. Vanessa felt the disconnection, and since her knee-jerk every time I obsessed was to shut down and run, which we will discuss later in the book, the gap got wider and wider. Every time I focused on our differences, I would be in my head and start to drift. My drift would cause her to drift, flipping the magnet and cracking trust. It felt like we were in a fight when we weren't.

I eventually realized what I was doing and how it was affecting the relationship. So one day I asked myself: Instead of resisting, defending, and trying to control or mold, what if I accept all our differences? Completely. Love it or leave it, as they say. I'm sure Vanessa wanted to say that to me every time she felt me being distant. What if instead of highlighting the contrast, I tried to find beauty in it? Answering that question—and by answering I mean putting action behind it—changed my life. Let me explain.

When I spotted a difference before, I would normally circle it with a red pen and lower the letter grade on our relationship. Now, when I noticed it, I sat with it, accepted it as fully as I could, and tried to find beauty in it. Could collecting a thousand gift cards, each with only about twenty cents on it, be cute? Could I appreciate her humor when it didn't match mine? Could I try to enjoy sex during the day (her thing) instead of at night?

As I practiced accepting our differences and finding the beauty in them, something interesting happened. I started to see the spirit of who Vanessa was. Instead of focusing on her tastes and behavior, I saw a whole person. This changed so much for me. The more I loved, respected, and admired her spirit, the less I was bothered by our differences. This recognition pulled me out of the trenches and allowed me to see the bigger picture, why I fell in love with her in the first place. I saw that I was with a whole person, not parts of a person. When I focused on the parts, I didn't appreciate the whole—the spirit of who Vanessa truly is. Because the whole is always greater than the parts. From here I started to find beauty in the contrast. Things that bothered me were now cute. Or if they weren't, they were not things I dwelled on anymore. By accepting, I was able to let go. By letting go, I was less in my head and more present. This kept Vanessa from running and flipped the magnet back. Now trust was created and a new love experience was given. To both of us.

I felt that I had come out the end of a dark tunnel and was trying to wave my hands as hard as I could at my client Drew to show her that she too could come through. That there was light here if she just changed her lenses. But she didn't listen and ended up breaking up with Marcus. She stopped seeing me, so I'm not sure how she is today. She did contact me once to tell me that she found someone else she had much more in common with, but then realized he didn't have what Marcus had. Maybe she eventually learned that accepting differences and finding beauty in the contrast would give her a new love experience, create new definitions, and ultimately bring about internal change. If not, she most likely has gone back to dating the same type of men (men without capacity), cementing her previous love experiences and beliefs about Self and stunting her growth.

Vanessa

From our first date I questioned if John was "into me" or not. The date ended with him awkwardly kissing not quite my cheek and not quite my mouth as I got in my car. The next day he sent me a sweet text that convinced me he was into it. But then he wouldn't sleep with me for what felt like *forever*, and I thought again that he wasn't into it. He was worried about our differences, about whether we were right for each other, and his constant worrying was affecting his ability to be present in our early relationship.

Both of those times, when he asked me if I knew why I was there and, if I did, how I knew, I told him, "I'm here because I ask myself *in the moment*, 'How do I feel? In this moment, do I feel happy? Yes. In this moment, am I enjoying our time together? Yes.' That is what I am basing it off of. I'm not thinking about whether we will be together forever or not. I'm thinking about, do I want to be here with you right now? And since the answer is 'yes,' I'm sitting here with you."

Practicing presence has always served me well. It can be an incredibly hard practice, but it's the only way I can tune into and trust my intuition—my "gut." If I can bring myself into my body and get very clear about what feelings and sensations are coming up in that exact moment, then I can act accordingly without overthinking it too much (easier said than done sometimes). In my early relationships, I didn't have this skill. I hadn't gone to therapy yet, I didn't have a yoga or meditation practice, I knew nothing about mindfulness or getting into my body, and I sure as hell didn't know about all my codependency shit, like people-pleasing, being the peacekeeper, and pretending to not have needs. Back then all of my relationship "choices" were based on my fight-or-flight responses, my unconscious, my upbringing, my reaction to past traumas, and my "logic." So it's not surprising that those relationships didn't last. I was constantly in my head. I had no idea what my intuition was really saying, and even if I did, I didn't have the tools to act on it.

There is a reason why mindfulness and mindfulness practices have exploded within the world of psychology in the past ten to twenty years. They work. Thousands of studies show that a mindfulness practice can help you reduce stress and anxiety, improve your cognition and attention, decrease your judgment of self and others, give you better emotional regulation, and even increase your immune function. Studies have also shown that a mindfulness practice can change you at a DNA level, by lengthening your telomeres (the little caps at the ends of your chromosomes that help protect them from damage). I could nerd out on the science of mindfulness all day, but instead I'll just say this: if I hadn't found yoga, meditation, and a therapist who worked from a spiritual place with a knowledge of mindfulness-based cognitive psychology, I would not be who I am today. These practices have altered my life in every way.

Most importantly for this conversation, a mindfulness practice has strengthened my skill at being present. It allows me to drop beneath the surface of the emotion or the reaction and question the why; to sit and watch the storm of a large feeling without acting on it; to connect what is happening in my body to what is happening in my mind; to be less judgmental and harsh with my partner and with myself; to self-soothe and regulate; and to not overstep and try to soothe or regulate my partner unless asked. (Trust me, the list could go on.)

Do John and I have a lot of differences? Yes. Do they drive me crazy? Yes. But I respect and value him as a person and resonate so deeply with what he is trying to build in this world that I've been willing to turn my logical side off and practice presence.

Even now, it's usually our differences that bring up a lot of resistance in me. When I focus on how loose he can be with details, how he doesn't always think things through before acting, how he would rather spend money on a new item than fix the item we already have, I can feel a wedge between us. Focusing this way makes me feel like it's me versus him, like I'm the only one looking out for our safety, like I do things the "right way" and he does them the "wrong way."

When I catch myself in this place, going around and around about our differences, I stop and breathe. I know that those stories about John and me are a way of trying to protect myself. If my logic can convince me that our differences are big enough to make me walk away, then I can dodge the possibility of being hurt, the possibility of ever being truly vulnerable, or the possibility that my way of doing things isn't always—*gasp*—the right way. My brain is trying to help me, but it does it using old patterns and habits based on survival. Meanwhile, my body, my gut, and my soul are all trying to help me expand, to be present with the discomfort, because that's the place where there's growth and healing and the potential for the deepest connection I have ever known. This is the voice I choose to listen to more closely now, because ultimately I know it won't steer me wrong.

* * *

There is a big difference between red flags and differences, just as there are between non-negotiables and preferences. Finding beauty in the contrast is about not allowing the things that bug you, the items on what we call your "preferences list," to become the reason you cut and run. Because cutting and running for that reason is usually coming from a place of fear, not from a place of connection and love.

Questions to Ask Yourself

Don't try to pretend that you and your partner don't have differences. That would be silly. We know you've gone over the list a million times in your head already. But if you are really struggling with those differences, it might be helpful to create a non-negotiables versus preferences list.

Take time to really think through the things that you would not compromise on. For example, not tolerating physical or verbal abuse should be obvious. But get more nuanced. Do you want a partner who doesn't get defensive and can take in and then act on feedback? Do you want a partner who verbally builds you up and makes you feel special? Do you want a partner who takes care of their body, mind, and spirit? Do you want a partner who has the same spiritual or religious beliefs and values as you?

If you find yourself listing things like a specific body type or "makes at least six figures," you've probably crossed over into preferences—nice-to-haves in an ideal world but not deal-breakers. Preferences can also be more serious things;

for example, Vanessa's preferences list included a partner who is also vegetarian or vegan and who is as passionate about social issues as she is. John is neither of these things, and that is okay with her.

Keep this list somewhere handy and refer to it often. It can, and probably should, evolve over time. Hold yourself accountable to not wavering on your non-negotiables, but also stay open to not seeing all of your preferences fulfilled by or reflected in the other person.

Those of you who struggle with codependent behaviors might have a really hard time actually making a list of what your desires and needs in a partner are. One of the biggest components of a codependent personality is a lack of trust in the Self, a lack of self-understanding and true self-knowledge. So if you find yourself struggling to come up with this list, work backward. What are some of the things you know you *don't* want in a partner based on experience? Use the process of elimination to create your list of non-negotiables. And remember, this list is not static—it can evolve and grow and change as you do. When Vanessa was first creating her list, she kept it in her phone so that she could reference it frequently and check in to see if it still felt "true," or if some things needed to be adjusted.

If you're interested in reading more about codependency, feel free to skip ahead to chapter 13, "Fuck *The Giving Tree*."

The Practice

One of the most common problems we have found that couples have is their inability to stay in the present—to "practice presence," as Vanessa says. We love in time machines: either we're comparing old love with new love and holding on to things from our previous love experiences, or we're future tripping and worried about all the what-ifs. Most commonly, we worry about whether this will last or whether we will get our heart broken—again.

The practice in staying present is to tune into what is coming up for you in the moment—again, without ignoring red flags or mismatched non-negotiables. It's about making it a habit to get out of your head and into your body. The next time you are sitting with your partner—or any person really—pause and go inward. What's happening in your body when you are with this person? Does your stomach feel tight or does it feel loose and relaxed? Is your breath shallow and in your upper chest, or do you find that your breathing feels slow and more in your belly? Are you on edge and calculating what you will say or do, or do you feel calm and relaxed and able to be yourself?

Start with these questions and see what else comes up for you. There are a lot of questions you could tap into in a practice of being present in your partnership. The point is to get really in tune with what your body is telling you when you are with your partner. Practicing presence can be a great way to tap into a sense of clarity around all the what-ifs coming from your head that otherwise would remain unanswerable.

CHAPTER 5

Love Like It's Going to End

John

I didn't know it at the time, but I needed Vanessa to hit pause on us the way she did after we got back from Costa Rica. Because I wouldn't have done it, and that speed bump gave me something. A revelation.

One Christmas my dad bought me a skateboard. I had been asking for one for over a year. Finally, it was here. But it wasn't what I had imagined in my head. It was wood color with no cool fancy graphics. It was wider and more expensive, almost like a skateboard for adults. I rejected it and pouted. "That's not what I wanted!" But he didn't take it back. It was this or nothing. So I kept it. And I rode it by myself because I didn't want the other kids to see it. But, I got sick of riding it by myself and buried it in my closet.

Then, a few months later, I had a random idea to turn my backyard into a roller coaster after my cousin complained about his parents never taking him to Disneyland because they didn't have money. Our house had a sidewalk that wrapped its way through the backyard and out the side. It was perfect. I staged cans to fall. Doors to open right before you hit them. All I needed was a "roller coaster"— something to push the neighborhood kids on. A normal skateboard was too small and skinny to use, but the one I had was perfect. Someone could sit on it cross-legged and not fall off because it was so much wider.

My cousin never came over to ride my "roller coaster," but I spent the entire summer pushing the neighborhood kids through my backyard. I had a dozen skateboards after that one as I got older and got into street skating. But that wide skateboard was my very first one and to this day my favorite. Because although it wasn't what I'd wanted, it was what I needed. I felt very alone at that time in my life. I was an introverted seven-year-old who spent too much time playing with Legos instead of making friends. After that summer, I made new friends. It was like the universe worked through my dad and flaky cousin, setting me up for a better school year. I stopped being isolated and started playing more with other kids. I learned that life has more to offer than just building things alone.

Vanessa taking a break from me for a week made me realize that this relationship was like that skateboard. It didn't match what I wanted, but there was something greater happening. And if I leaned into it, I knew I was meant to learn something. Not just about myself, but about love and what I put weight on. This experience would give me new lenses. And it would finally allow me to walk across the great divide, from old love to new.

NEW LOVE

Love is about the belief, not the promise. So many want the promise. So many crave a contract. So many want a guarantee. But love is not property, like it was in the fifties, when life revolved around building the perfect picket fence, wearing dresses and pressed suits, having 2.5 kids, and walking on eggshells.

Love is a space. And in that space, a belief is born. The action of love is wrapped around that belief. Like arms. And that action, assuming it's healthy, protects the space where the belief continues to grow.

You will create the space to believe if you focus more on the belief—the expansion, the possibilities, the greater that comes from two whole people, and the glue and growth of today, not tomorrow—and less on the deal, the agreement, and all the what-ifs. If you love *with* instead of *at* or *around*. If you stay engaged in the here and now, lock eyes, and hold faces. Gently and long enough to see deeper, past your past. If you refuse to play chess and just be—the most honest version of yourself. If you seek to be seen instead of wanted. As you feed and grow that space, the promise will be the fruit.

To love is to create the space to believe.

Without it, love will bear no promise.

We, like you, have put the promise first. We, like you, have grabbed instead of held. And we, like you, have lost.

Engagement is about being fully present and seen. It's two people farming the soil, with awareness and ownership, with transparency, connection, and distance. Championing each other's whole story, not just a chapter. Looking beyond skin. Loving with eyes closed and palms open. It's no longer just about the picket fence. Because we all know that shit has splinters.

We, like you, have loved with only our eyes. We, like you, exchanged vows for security and a false permanence as a way to control. And we, like you, have lost.

The new love? That is compassion and honesty over time lines and promises. Focusing on depth instead of width. Letting go of what was, including the blueprints and old folded and creased definitions from our parents that we still keep in our back pockets. Leaning into something new without strings, new love that stems from courage, not fear. Courage to speak truth and accept differences, understanding that pain is not a reason to blame, but a part of love. Like discoloration on a leaf. Courage to show shortcomings and weaknesses. To sit still in and through. To hold on to yourself before holding on to the other. And if the other drops to their knees, to not drop with them but to stay standing, offering a hand, not a life.

The new love is purpose driven, not ego driven. Greater than the parts. The new love comes in moments. Moments that stand alone and are not defined by years. The new love redefines beauty as how the other makes you feel, not just as attraction and your preferred aesthetics. The new love is about a beautiful person, not beautiful people, and it examines energy, flow, and the spiritual dance. The new love is a slow burn. Not lightning in a cracked bottle.

The new love is about the micro. Like dimples and freckles and beauty marks in imperfect places. A crooked smile, off-center banter, and idiosyncrasies that make the dynamic truly dynamic. The quick glance. The new love is not about the finish but about discovery. The new love is about putting value in the power of the collision of two stories and the secondary change produced from that collision. It's not how many years it lasts. Because length doesn't equal potency. Or high notes. We all know this.

The new love is about the ability to make both parties feel supported and heard and seen and safe without fists and a puffed-out chest. The new love is about building something together that doesn't fit in a box but sits on a table as a centerpiece. The new love is about embracing instead of trying to change. Growing individually over just growing old together. It's about the daily ride. A new way to fight that doesn't create panic or cut you off at the knees. The new love is about communication and taking all your ideas about types, attraction, and what a "good" relationship looks like, every judgment you've made because of your past, and starting with just one thing—curiosity.

One of the most powerful ways to not react to your partner is to pull from curiosity. Curiosity dissolves reactions. Curiosity encourages exploration and slaps down judgment. Curiosity is the bridge we rarely walk across. We're too busy building walls and coming up with our defense. So pull from curiosity daily. It's what creates a new love.

Vanessa

To love like it's going to end is a reckoning. A reckoning with the undeniable reality that life ends. That none of this is promised. That I can live until I'm 100 and die peacefully in my sleep, or I can walk outside and get hit by a bus tomorrow. If I knew, without a doubt, that tomorrow was my last day on Earth, then how would I want to love today? Not just live, but love. Because loving *is* living.

So many of us, myself included, live our lives in the past or the future. We struggle with loss of control and the unknown, and so our minds are constantly trying to plan ahead, to get in front of the existential feeling of dread deep in our psyche that we truly do not know what will happen tomorrow. Living in the future (in the promise) creates anxiety, while living in the past pulls us into depressive states and lower frequencies. There is a reason why mindfulness and meditation have finally gotten the scientific support they deserve. When we strengthen our ability to stay present through mindfulness and meditative practices, we pull ourselves out of the future and the past and land in the now. We enhance our ability to smell the fragrance of the jasmine blooming in the spring, our ability to notice the vibrancy of the colors in the sunset, our ability to feel an actual warmth in our body when our child laughs or our partner gives us a look from across the kitchen. To me, this is what John means when he says focus on depth instead of width.

I'm not pushing you to become a monk who sits in lotus position for hours each day in silence. I'm pushing you to develop short and easy mindful practices that will strengthen your awareness muscle. I'm pushing you to strengthen this muscle so that you don't miss it. What is *it*? Your life. The individual moments that create joy and yet are the ones we so often miss because we're moving too fast and worrying too much about the next thing. Love like it's going to end. Because it is.

Questions to Ask Yourself

How can you start to put weight and focus on deeper things in your relationship? What are some of the unspoken, or maybe unseen, things you haven't given your attention to that you can start noticing and sitting with?

What would a new love look like for you? A new love doesn't have to be with a new person, it can be a new love with the same person. By slowing down and intentionally bringing mindfulness into your relationship(s), how can you start to change the way you see love?

Are you pulling from curiosity or from judgment and defense? Are you tracing old love blueprints or creating new ones? Are you practicing compassion and honesty or focusing on time lines and promises?

If you can love again, knowing everything you know about love but without the fears and insecurities from past love experiences, what would that look like?

The Practice

- Stop right now and look around. Notice three things. Don't just notice them, but really see them. Color, texture, detail. Get up and examine them more closely if you can.

- Now close your eyes and inhale deeply. Notice any smells, good or bad. Focus on the smell. Is it pungent, sweet, intense, faint, or lingering? Does it bring up any images or connections in your mind as you focus on it?

- Keep your eyes closed and now bring your attention to any sounds around you. Focus on the sounds that are far away, in the distance. Now notice whatever sound is closest to you. Traffic, the hum of the AC, the dishwasher, a dog breathing, *you* breathing.

- Now shift your awareness to the feeling of your body in your chair. Can you feel the weight of yourself pushing down into your seat? The connection point between your back and the chair? What about where the backs of your legs touch?

- Finally, smack your lips and mouth a few times. What is the taste that is the most recent and present on your tongue? Did you have coffee? Can you still taste breakfast? What about a kiss from your partner?

This exercise is called The Five Senses. It is available to us all of the time. When you find yourself moving too quickly, obsessing about details and the future, stop and go through each of the senses. Don't let your mind tell you that you don't have time. This exercise takes about three minutes total, so *everyone* has the time to do it. If you struggle with being mindful, just know that it's your mind's job to think and worry. It doesn't want to stop doing that, so it's going to make it difficult for you to be present. This is normal.

Presence is the foundation of creating a new love experience. Practice being present in life and you will become more present in love.

PART 2

Swim Past the Breakers

CHAPTER 6

Swim Past the Breakers

John

Now I was in. Fully. No more ambivalence. No more hot and cold, with one foot in the past and one foot in the future. Both feet were planted in the here and now. We even moved in together. And when any new couple moves in together relatively quickly, shit can hit the fan.

Living with someone is a big deal. The little things in daily life that bother each of you become stones in the relationship shoe. But strangely, they didn't bother me. The voodoo dolls made of hair that Vanessa collected from the drain and slapped on the shower wall didn't gross me out. I thought that was kind of cute. The way she shot daggers at me like she was going to murder me in my sleep if I ate her leftovers wasn't that big a deal. I understood that food was one of her love languages. Standing up like Linda Blair in *The Exorcist* and yelling strange shit (sleep talking) in the middle of the night, yes, that scared the shit out of me, but

I got used to it with the help of earplugs and Klonopin. And finally, the hardest thing I had to swim past was the way she scratched my back.

Now let me explain. Back scratches for me are a must. It's not an ego thing. I literally can't scratch my back due to poor flexibility and back muscles. Also, for some reason my back is constantly itchy, so if my partner doesn't scratch it for me, I have to find a tree and do it like a bear. So this was a big deal, something I should have expressed when we first met. But I didn't need to because in the beginning her scratches were hard and thorough. But over time her fingers became soft water streams from a broken sprinkler. I tried to be empathetic and understand that skin under her nails grossed her out, something she had not expressed to me when we first met. I tried to not file this under false advertising, which would fuel ambivalence—the old John Kim. So I bought a wide wooden Korean back scratcher and that was that. Everything was good. We were swimming along.

Until we hit a wall. A big one. Vanessa got pregnant. It was something we didn't expect. Came out of nowhere. She was on birth control. How did this happen? I was finally getting traction with my career. Books and speaking gigs and a growing podcast. The last thing I wanted was a child. Hell no was I going to be the dad mistaken for her grandfather when I picked her up from high school. Because seventeen years from now I would be sixty-three! And if you go by my Korean age (which says you're one when you're born), I would be sixty-fucking-four! Fuck. That. Kids were not in my blueprint.

When I was in my early twenties, I got my girlfriend

pregnant. We were just kids. We didn't know what to do. We didn't have any tools. We could barely take care of ourselves, let alone a child. I told her I would support whatever decision she made. I remember the cold morning when I drove her to the clinic. It felt empty, apocalyptic. I was scared. Sad. There was an eerie silence the entire day. After the procedure, she was different. There was an emptiness in her eyes that never really went away. I didn't want to go through that again. After some discussion, Vanessa and I decided we were going to keep it.

Although Vanessa never wanted kids either, she felt like she, and we, were in a place in our lives where we could take this on and make it work. We actually started to get excited about it. Could this be the new love experience the universe wanted me to have? I never considered raising a child with someone before. I could imagine it bringing a closeness that couldn't be produced otherwise. There was no ambivalence this time. I accepted it fully. Hearing a heartbeat flash-forwarded scenes of all the things my dad never did with me. I was excited about being a dad. For the first time in my life.

Then we hit another wall. This one nearly ended our relationship. It was the first time I felt the kind of pain where nothing matters. It felt like that day I drove my girlfriend to the clinic. But times ten. We would have to heal from this together or our relationship wouldn't last.

We lost the baby.

Vanessa

Moving in together hadn't been something we were even discussing. I loved living alone in my little apartment in the valley. It was the first time in my life I had ever had my own place. I liked the separation and distance it created in the relationship. I also liked that I could retreat when I needed to or when things got tough.

But about eight months into the relationship, I got pregnant. On birth control. Yes, it happens. I was so clear up until that moment that I never wanted kids. I always felt like I wanted to just be the cool aunt who traveled and brought home fun gifts to her nieces and nephews and friends' kids. My brother and sister are much younger than me, so I had gotten a very clear crash course in what having kids really looks like, and I was adamant that this was not part of my life plan.

We considered our options and after a lot of discussion and inner turmoil decided that at this stage in our lives, having a kid was something we could presumably handle. We both took a deep breath and prepared to buckle up for a massive shift in everything we knew.

I told my family and my close friends. Everyone was shocked, but happy. John and I started talking about the details, and about moving in together. I told him I was totally fine living alone with the baby and him coming over when he could to help, but John insisted, and so we started looking at places.

Then, at eight weeks, I started cramping and felt nauseous. I knew something was off. It was as if one minute I felt pregnant and the next I just didn't. I took myself to the ER and waited until a bed opened up. The doctor confirmed what I already knew. By that time John was there, lying beside me in the tiny bed. "I'm sorry," I said to him, while we both cried. He cried big tears, and his shoulders bobbed. I, on the other hand, felt numb. I was disappointed but didn't actually feel sad.

Over the next few weeks, as I went to multiple doctor's appointments to make sure my body was healing properly without intervention, every time I was in my car coming home I felt anger. Not sadness. I was angry at my body because it had let me down. I took care of myself, I ate healthy, I worked out, I had come so far in my emotional work and spiritual growth, and it felt like the universe, higher power, source, whatever you wanted to call it, was punishing me in some way. I don't think these feelings ever went away. I had to work hard to grieve and process my anger, first alone and in therapy, and then with John.

He didn't understand my anger, and I couldn't connect with him in his sadness. It felt like we were really disconnected in our grieving process, and I felt very misunderstood. It was as if each of us thought the other was somehow abnormal in their process, and because we couldn't understand each other's process, we got defensive. It was a really hard time for us. There were a lot of nights we went to bed upset with each other. But through a lot of conversations, even ones we didn't want to have, we each found our way toward accepting where the other was coming from, even if we didn't necessarily understand it. It was a huge lesson in trying to understand before being understood.

As we started to again feel close, closer actually than we had felt before, we talked again about kids. Was the universe simply saying this wasn't in the cards for us, or that having a kid wasn't the right path? We didn't know the answer but decided not to get back on birth control and just see what happened. If it was meant to be, it would be, right?

Six months later I was deep into the second day of a three-day meditation retreat that I had gifted myself for my birthday. I was alone, with no distractions, and had finally dropped "beneath the surface" (as we say in meditation about finally feeling calm, not twitchy, and like time no longer means anything) when I had one of the clearest "knowings" I have ever felt. "I want this. I want to have a baby *with John*. I want to do this with *him*. Not with anyone else." My eyes popped open and my heart sped up.

When my mom asked me early on in our relationship about the possibility of a family, I told her there was something different about John. I didn't see myself having kids at that point, but I did know, deep in my bones, that John was the type of man who would be a good father regardless of what happened with our relationship. Meaning, if we split up after having a child, it wouldn't affect how much he loved and showed up for his child. I had personally experienced the reality of a father who could not do that, which always made me feel like I had been punished for being 50 percent my mother's DNA.

Two days after the retreat I was home and crying while John and I sat on the bed together and I told him about my knowing. I was squirming in discomfort from how vulnerable it felt to share this, but I had to tell him. I wasn't ambivalent anymore. I knew. And yet, we had not been using protection for over six months and nothing had happened.

Now I was sad, I was hurting. I actually wanted this and what if I couldn't get pregnant?

That same week we rented a cabin in the woods so John could work on his second book. We were disconnected from everything and everyone, in the snow, writing and reading and making love. Four weeks later, the stick confirmed it—I was pregnant.

THE BREAKERS

> *I'm so thankful I didn't end up with what I thought I wanted.*
>
> **—SO MANY PEOPLE WHO FINALLY SWIM PAST THE BREAKERS**

In the ocean, the breakers are the turbulent waves that come crashing onto the shore. Like the sunrise and sunset, they are consistent and never ending. The thing is, if you never swim past them, you will not know that most of the ocean is actually calm and peaceful. You will only know the ocean to be turbulent and chaotic.

Relationships also have breakers. And if you never swim past them, you will not know calm and peace, nor will you be able to build a healthy and sustainable relationship. Instead, the turbulence will leave you exhausted, and as though you were fighting a riptide you will eventually drown—by leaving the relationship, sabotaging it, or mentally and emotionally checking out. Not swimming past the breakers is a common reason why relationships fall apart.

So what are the breakers? Simply put, the breakers are when things get hard, when reality hits, when the love story that looked so exciting in the trailer turns into the documentary. The breakers are anything that creates resistance. They may be surface things, like different love languages, communication styles, opinions, and definitions. Or they may be deeper issues, like your emotional reactions triggered by your partner and the relationship, which we will get into shortly. The breakers are *not* to be confused with mistreatment, aggression, abuse, or actions from people who use our wounds against us. There is a difference between a breaker and a red flag. The former brings us growth and a bridge to a deeper relationship with the Self; the latter is a barrier to growth and in direct opposition to a connection with the Self.

The truth is, love doesn't actually start until things get hard. Because the easy part isn't love. The easy part is lust, infatuation, the honeymoon phase, and the feeling we get lost in when someone new kisses us back. The easy part is the exciting discovery phase before we see anything wrong or unhealthy. Before the new lens, the revelations, the realization of how much work it takes to build a healthy, sustainable relationship. The easy part is not love. It's hope, and a lot of the time it's false hope. Love happens after you swim past all of that—the breakers.

Here are some common breakers to notice and try to swim past:

1. **The sticky relationship dynamic:** This is the unhealthy, unconscious attempt to repair an old wound that we discussed in part 1. These types of connections

usually create a turbulent cycle, a mini-relationship with a beginning, middle, and end. An extreme example is the domestic violence cycle of an abusive relationship: the honeymoon stage → the buildup (increase in tension) → the stand-over (control, fear) → the explosion → the remorse (justification, minimization, guilt) → the pursuit (fear of losing, promises) → the honeymoon stage → and over and over again.

The sticky relationship dynamic itself can be unhealthy, stunting growth for both parties. "But he's not abusive," "But I know he (she) loves me"—these are the types of excuses we tell ourselves or our friends for why we stay in this relationship. We don't realize it's less about the person and more about the relationship dynamic created by two people with unhealed wounds. Eventually one of them taps out. Eventually one of them has had enough. Eventually one of them wants to heal from their wounds. When this happens, the relationship starts to fall apart, since one person is now outgrowing the other. The unconscious bond stretches and eventually breaks.

There is a spectrum of sticky relationships: again, an abusive relationship would be an extreme example. Hints of codependency can be sticky. Hints of jealous behavior and subtle control can be sticky. Hints of a distancer-and-pursuer dynamic can be sticky. Hints of the desire for drama can be sticky. Any relationship dynamic that creates unhealthy behavior and patterns is sticky. Healthy relationships are usually non-stick. But if we have done little work on ourselves, we are usually attracted to sticky relationships and repelled by the non-stick. That's why we must swim past the breakers, "the sticky," to get to a healthy, non-stick relationship dynamic. And we must sit in the place where we find ourselves after we swim past the breakers. It will be uncomfortable there, maybe something we label as boring or lacking chemistry. We must sit in that place until it becomes the norm. Until we recondition our bodies and the relationship dynamic we are attracted to changes. Until we become repelled by the sticky instead of attracted to it.

2. **The contrast:** All of our differences and how they make us question if we are with the right person. When the honeymoon feeling starts to fade and the image we have of our partner doesn't match who they really are, we get anxious. We feel confused. The fantasy is gone. Reality has arrived. This happens often in long-distance relationships, since every meeting is a honeymoon and no one can do anything wrong. When we start to really get to know someone, seeing all sides of them, their stains, their shortcomings, their edges, and no longer just seeing the movie poster, we are in the breakers. This is where many drift and wonder if they made the right choice. This is where a lot of people bounce without doing any work or giving the relationship a fair shot.

3. **The little things that bother us:** The stepping on each other's shoes as we learn how to do the dance of life together and live together. The way he doesn't make the

bed right, or at all. The fact that she runs the dishwasher with only three plates and a fork. The little hairs he leaves in the sink after shaving. The coffee grounds she always forgets to clean up. The empty shampoo bottle he never throws away. Her dirty socks on the floor. The chip bag always being open, the cereal box never closed. The way she always runs late. The way he forgets where he put the car keys when she's running late. All the little things that can become big when we start doing life with someone. All these daily life things can add up to a giant crowbar that splits people apart.

4. **Our emotional triggers:** Strong emotional reactions that come up for us in reaction to our partner and the relationship interactions. They are usually tied to our story and sometimes don't have anything to do with the other person. Maybe he forgets to text you, like the ex-boyfriend who cheated on you, so you think he's being unfaithful too. Maybe she talks to you in a way that subtly reminds you of your mother. Maybe you shut down because he raises his voice when you guys have an argument like your dad did while you were growing up. We have to be aware of what's emotionally activating us, why that's happening, and then attempt to work through it so we are not constantly just reacting to each other. Reactions cause bonfires.

If we follow the thread of reaction, what we can eventually see is that it usually stems from some kind of old hurt or wound. So our defenses go up to protect us. And when defenses go up, there is no room for compassion and understanding. This isn't just therapy speak, this is actually neuroscience. When we get defensive, our fight-or-flight response is activated. And when that happens, our prefrontal cortex (the part of our brain responsible for thinking, empathy, reason, logic) goes dark. So instead of coming together, we are pushing our partner away, spraying the fire with lighter fluid, and not learning anything about the wound that actually needs to be healed, or recognizing that the relationship itself could help with the healing. These unexamined reactions cause relationships to fall apart.

Prefrontal cortex: The youngest section of the brain in humans and primates, responsible for empathy, logic, and language. When we are in a heightened emotional state or a state of stress, access to the cortex can be restricted or sometimes impossible as the brain goes into "fight or flight." It is then only able to access the limbic (emotional) or the reptilian portion of the brain. When this happens we are only acting from a state of survival.

John
I'M NOT USED TO A PRIUS

Remy was in a brand-new relationship. Again. But this one was different. She didn't just allow things to happen based on butterflies, which usually turn into bats. She made a conscious choice to break the pattern of being with "bad boys." She wanted to stop the chase, the games, the manipulation, the cheating, the lack of taking ownership. She was in her thirties now and wanted something safe and stable. She wanted to be in something for more than two years, to build something lasting. She was sick of having to go through her boyfriend's phone and convince herself that he would change. But there was a problem. Her new choice was wise but not exciting. She "traded in a vintage Mustang for a Prius." Well, at least that's how she described it.

As we processed this new relationship, Remy realized that her body wasn't used to calm and healthy. It was used to the dopamine from the highs and the anxiety of the lows of an emotional roller-coaster ride. Uncertainty was all she knew. From the time she could walk, the sky was always falling. Mom and Dad would fight. Dad would leave. Mom would cry and curse him out and drink. Dad would come back. The world was safe again, until it wasn't. Love meant chaos and uncertainty—this was the blueprint she traced as she grew up. Without knowing it. Remy was addicted to the feeling of finding something after it's been lost.

So when she finally decided to date someone healthy, she didn't lose him. He was there. He was present. He listened to her, remembered how she liked her eggs, and put water on her nightstand every night before going to bed. He did the kinds of things she should have been bragging about with her girlfriends during their weekly brunch, which her last ex hadn't allowed her to attend. But she didn't brag. His behavior made her cringe. It was confusing. Logically

Remy knew that he was good to her, and that this was what healthy love should look like. But this was all new to her body. And it reacted like a kid who's given peas and throws them at the wall—she tried to sabotage, instigate, and push him away. But she had something in this relationship that she didn't have in others—a therapist.

Remy came every week, and we processed everything that was being stirred up. We explored how she felt and where it might be coming from so she wouldn't just re-act to that feeling. She was given homework to sit in what was uncomfortable and unfamiliar. It wasn't easy. She tried to end the relationship many times. Almost had an affair. Twice. But she sat in the discomfort, in what for her was "the boring."

I reminded her that these were the breakers and that she needed to swim past them. She was confused because she thought "breakers" meant only the contrasts between two people, the stepping on each other's toes as they really got to know each other—aka moving in with each other. But I reminded her that anything uncomfortable can be the breakers. It doesn't have to be total chaos. In her case, the calm was the breakers. So she stayed in it. Not white-knuckling her way through it but breathing and creating space for revelations. And slowly but surely, her body be-came acclimated to this new love. It finally put its guard down and became less reactive. Instead, her body was now curious and willing. It learned something brand-new—the safe space created by trust. For the first time in her life, Remy didn't have to fake her orgasms.

I related to my client. But I was doing exactly what I told her not to do. Resisting. Running away. Swimming toward the shore instead of past the breakers. Not sitting in discomfort and reconditioning my body to have a new love experience. Instead, I was trying to trace old love patterns that were etched into my body like my morning coffee routine. The experience with Vanessa was new and foreign. I was craving the comfort of the old. But doing sessions with this client, who was struggling with the same thing, made me aware of what was happening in my own life and put action behind my words. She made me accountable without even knowing it. I didn't want to be a hypocrite. I should have been paying her for our sessions.

I'm not going to lie and tell you I'm sipping margaritas on a pool raft in a state of bliss because I swam past old love tracks laid since high school. I often fall into a riptide and get dragged under. It's been four years and I still have hard days when this new type of relationship triggers me and constantly holds up a mirror. Some days I'm exhausted from swimming and just want the tide to take me.

But it's also better these days. Easier. I have moments when my body takes a breath and smiles at me, thanking me for giving it something new and good for it. It's the same smile etched into my face on the way home after a really hard workout. I see the island this time. And it's not a mirage created by Disney movies, young love, and advertising. I know this long swim is what loving someone looks like. And I know being in the resistance gets easier. Because my love buds are changing, if you were to ask me what relationship was the healthiest, it would be this one. I also know Vanessa is swimming as well, right next to me. That knowing is new, and it gives me daily strength to keep swimming.

Vanessa

> When you're dating, each person you meet is a practice partner. You get to practice showing up, being curious, present, and open.
>
> —MELANIE HERSCH, LMFT, DATING COACH

You're probably asking, as I did when I first started working with the concept of swimming past the breakers, what the difference is between the breakers and red flags. How do I know that my gut isn't just telling me that I should move on?

If swimming past the breakers has a goal, it's to learn. It's to grow and deepen your understanding of *yourself*. It's to break old patterns and create more emotional resiliency. And it's to learn how to respond instead of react to your own emotional triggers. Okay, so maybe there are many goals.

Dating is a lot like job hunting. Have you ever been told before an interview to remember that "you're interviewing them as much as they're interviewing you"? Each person you date, like a potential new job, is going to offer something different. Each one is going to have different compensation packages and PTO structures. The culture of each is going to be different, like the commute time and the number of flexible work-from-home days the job offers. None of the people you date will be bad or good, better or worse, but each will be different and worthy of exploring to see how well they fit with you and your expectations, needs, desires, and goals. As with people, you don't get to an understanding of the nuances of a job without asking and digging. Some of the information is offered up front—here it is, take it or leave it. But some of it, like workplace culture, needs to be dug up, experienced in the heat of the moment. You need to experience the real real. Not the shiny one-liner the employer puts on their website about how "community and building safe environments are what we're all about. Plus we're dog friendly!"

I don't mean to sound like I think people are disposable or don't have depth to them. But if we went into dating more like we approach trying to find a fulfilling job, most of us would probably stick around a little longer and do a little more exploring before we bailed. With a job, you have an initial idea of what it is based on the interview, but until you're in the heat of the moment you can't truly *know* it.

Everyone puts on a shiny face when they start a job *or* go on a first or second date. Even on date three, you are probably not going to know if this person is someone you could marry and live with for forty years. You might have butterflies and be insanely attracted to them (which might be enough to schedule a fourth date), or you might be totally repulsed by who they voted for in the last election (which might be enough to delete their number from your phone before dinner is even over). But truly *knowing* another person, really swimming past the breakers, takes time. Especially considering that the breakers are actually more about you than anyone else.

Let's say you decide you want to go on a fourth, fifth, tenth date with this person. Things are feeling pretty good between you two. A month in, they come to you with feedback about how something you said the night before felt really dismissive of their feelings and, honestly, a bit condescending. Your face gets hot. You feel the defensiveness rising. You pull in. Inside your head you're thinking, "They don't *get* me and my humor. Red flag. I didn't *mean* to be condescending, I was just being me. I was *joking*. We're obviously not meant for each other."

This is a breaker.

You have two choices at this point: You can say "screw it" and stumble back to shore, coughing and sputtering out the water that the breaking waves have inevitably shoved up your nose. Or you can think, "Oh, this is interesting. This person is telling me that something I said has hurt their feelings and I'm getting defensive. I notice how hot my face is getting and how I want to lash out and make it their fault rather than apologize. I wonder what that's about. I'll try to understand before being understood. Try to understand before being understood. Try to understand before being understood. Let me sit and breathe for a second until I can get myself a bit more grounded. Then I'll ask them more about their experience rather than reacting out of fear and defensiveness." This is when you center yourself, cough the water out, push your hair out of your face, and dive under the next wave in order to get a little farther out into the calm water. (By the way, this is what happened in real life when I found myself in rough water. It's also the dialogue that happens in my head just about every time there is conflict between John and me—*still*.)

Each time one of these moments presents itself to you (and any intimate relationship will have many many such moments), you have a choice. To react like you always have, or to respond differently this time. Each time you respond instead of react, each time you pause and examine what is coming up for you—the why, the part you can own, the part you should maybe be speaking up about but aren't—you are swimming a little farther past the breakers. Swimming past the breakers doesn't mean, again, that you've found your forever person. It means you are practicing. You are using this moment in this relationship as a springboard for your inner growth, which is going to benefit you and *any* person you are in a relationship with.

If you are basing your entire decision to stick around in a relationship on whether or not you feel butterflies and always feel understood and not challenged or pushed back on, you are in for a long and, honestly, lonely life. Not just in romance but in any chosen relationship. I've spent far too much of my life being a people-pleaser—doing or not doing things, saying or not saying things, whatever it took. Now I've committed to getting more familiar with conflict in all my relationships. Do I enjoy it? No, of course not. But this isn't about enjoyment (at least not all of the time). It's about a deepening. It's about real intimacy and vulnerability. I'm sick of surface relationships that always end up feeling un-fulfilling and laced with resentment. I'm ready for the real shit. The feeling that comes after you have just duked out a major conflict or have had to face the fact that something you did or said was actually really hurtful and completely not okay in an adult relationship, the feeling when you're on the other side, standing side by side, feeling closer and more in sync than you were an hour before (or maybe twenty-four, depending on the length of the fight!). I'll take that exhausted but exhilarated feeling of having swum past yet another breaker any day over the alternative of standing on the shore looking out at what could have been or what I long for.

Questions to Ask Yourself

First, it starts with awareness. What do the breakers look like for you in your current relationship? What do they feel like? What is bringing you resistance in your relationships? What has brought you resistance in past relationships? This question can be asked about any relationship, not just roman-tic ones. When have you reacted and then wished later you had acted differently? When has something someone said or did brought up an emotion so strong and overwhelming in you that it felt all-consuming? Can you remember having a similar feeling at another moment in your life with someone else, probably when you were younger? Can you remember having a similar reaction?

What about the contrast? Can you look at the differences between you and your partner as what makes you comple-mentary rather than incompatible? In what areas do your partner's strengths make up for your weaknesses?

We have to ask ourselves every day: Which of the things that annoy us about each other are worth speaking up about? Which things are part of our partner's personality and in the grand scheme of things are not really that important, but may be what we're using as an excuse to bail when things get too hard? Vanessa would say here that any annoyance that leaves us with a lingering feeling of resentment is worth speaking up about, but understanding that it's not about the specific thing that annoys us—it's about what it causes us to feel, how it makes us feel unsafe, unlovable, overlooked, dismissed, taken for granted, etc.

For example, John knows it means a lot to Vanessa if he puts a glass of water on her nightstand when he gets his own glass before bed. Since her love language is acts of service, she interprets only getting himself water as not loving her. It's such a simple thing. If he's getting himself a glass of water anyway, why shouldn't he get her one as well? But John doesn't think it's that big a deal. So if Vanessa doesn't express what this act means to her, he probably won't make an effort to do it every time. Then, over time, Vanessa's anger and resentment grows and most likely comes out on a random day when he forgot to buy the mustard. It's not about the water. It's about feeling unloved.

The Practice

The practice here has two parts. The first starts with this question: What feeling is signaling that you have a need that is not being expressed? Sit with that question and try to follow the thread back to the origin of your reactions. The origins are sometimes the breakers themselves. It's important to remember, if you can, specific examples of when you had a similar emotional response, but also to get really clear on the *specific* emotions you remember having. Shame? Being overwhelmed? Confusion? Nervousness? Violation? Inferiority? Helplessness? Try to stay away from the catchall emotional terms: happy, mad, glad, sad. Go deeper.

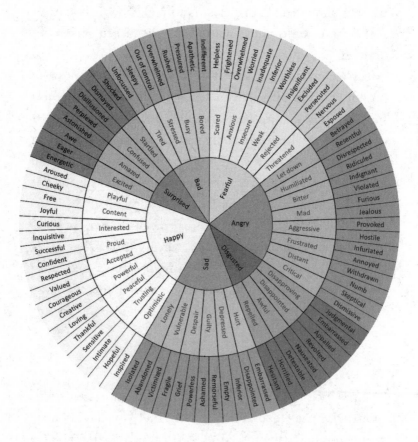

Once you've pinpointed a few of those primary emotions, turn up your awareness dial on when and where they come up in your life now and your current relationships. How you responded to those feelings *then* is probably how you are responding to them *now*. Are you exploding in anger? Are you shutting down in shame? Are you walking on eggshells and swallowing the big emotion entirely out of fear of rejection or abandonment?

The second part is to try to be open about how you are reacting, to name it, and then, once you name it, to see if you can stay open to responding in a different way. This is how you swim past the breakers. So, for example, if you shut down when you feel ashamed, see if you can stay present by doing mindful breathing or repeating a mantra ("Try to understand before being understood," for example). If you feel like you're about to explode, ask for a minute to go take care of yourself and soothe your nervous system so you can come back feeling calmer.

Remember, love doesn't start until it gets hard. Swim past the breakers. Calm is on the other side. There you can finally start to build something real. And lasting.

CHAPTER 7

Love without Your Past

There's another common pitfall that many fall into that keeps their relationship stuck and both parties stunted. Unless we're aware of our past love experiences and their impact on our current relationship and are actively working on dissolving any lasting issues, the past will stain our present relationship. Once you swim past the breakers, you must love without your past.

Just because you're not thinking about your ex all the time doesn't mean you're not carrying some kind of residue from that love experience. Usually it's unconscious, running underneath our awareness. So first, we must become aware. Bring the residue of past experiences into the light to investigate and explore. Then follow the thread down to find out where that residue comes from.

And finally, work on processing, confronting, and dissolving it.

Let's now explore some of the things that may be rippling into the new from the old.

THE RELATIONSHIP DANCE YOU HAD WITH AN EX

Every relationship has a dance. The banter, the back-and-forth, the syncing up. Not just what the two of you have in common but how you are with each other, whether it's humor, language, mannerisms, energy, how you work together. Subtle or obvious, every relationship has its own rhythm and cadence. And it's different for every relationship because every person is different.

Like many people, you may have loved by trying to replicate in your current relationship the dance you had with someone else. This tracing from the past is unfair to your partner and also damaging. You can start to believe your partner isn't right for you because you don't share the same dynamic you once had with someone else. But that would be impossible, not just because you're with someone else but because *you* are someone else. You're not who you used to be when you felt the magic with "the one" in college. Replicating that relationship dynamic is impossible. You're running toward a mirage, blindfolded. And now you're in your head instead of in the relationship and not allowing a new dance to form. You are chasing what *was* instead of accepting and building on what *is*. To love without your past, you must remove your blindfold or you won't see what's right underneath your nose.

OLD LOVE BLUEPRINTS

When we were younger, our hearts were fresh powdered snow. But having our hearts broken over and over again hardened us. We trusted less, feared more, and became less open to new definitions than when we were young. Now love is imprinted on patchy ice.

For most of us, our younger love experiences were probably the unhealthiest. We didn't have a solid sense of Self. We loved only with our hearts, not with our heads. We were walking reactions and didn't have any tools. So the definitions of love we carried into adulthood were often distorted and damaging. They created cracks in our relationship container, preventing relationships from growing and thriving.

Here's the problem. Definitions are wrapped in shoulds. Some of these definitions tell us what intimacy *should* look like. What sex *should* be like. How our partner *should* treat us. What our partner *should* say and buy us on our birthday. How we *should* celebrate our anniversary. What we *should* and *shouldn't* disclose to each other. How we *should* act, smell, dress, and on and on and on. These shoulds, formed by upbringing, society, and previous relationships, can build a fence around our current relationship, walling it off from what it could be.

ANGER AND RESENTMENT

If you have loved, you have been hurt. If you have not resolved this hurt in some way, there's a good chance you are still harboring some anger, which may have turned into resentment. And this resentment, whether you know it or not, is affecting your current relationship. How? you ask. However you were hurt before will be your hot stove—a sensitive area. You will not want to touch it even if you know it's not on.

For example, say your ex-boyfriend, the one you thought you were going to marry and have beautiful babies with, cheated on you in college and you never processed it; you just pushed it down and moved on, getting into another relationship as fast as you could. And of course that one didn't work out because you had some new trust issues you couldn't quite manage. So you moved on again, without ever starting the journey of forgiveness for your first ex. Now, in your current relationship, any hint of possible dishonesty—maybe he doesn't text you back right away, or he forgets to call when he's out with friends—will trigger an overreaction. Being on edge like this prevents the building of trust that allows you to love from a distance. You are loving with an old blueprint.

We have to work to understand and heal past hurts so we don't bring them into the present. If we don't, we'll love with fear and uncertainty. We'll be on edge and untrusting, loving around our partner instead of with them.

BELIEFS ABOUT YOURSELF

Some of the most damaging takeaways from past relationships are the false beliefs we are left with about ourselves. We internalize what happened, believing that if only *we* were different it would have been different. If the relationship was unhealthy it's easy to leave it thinking there is something wrong with us. Breaking up was not just our fault—it was because of who we are, or how we are. We are defective. Unlovable. There is something wrong with us. We don't have the ability to love or to be loved in a healthy way.

Or the opposite! Sometimes we're left believing there is something wrong with the other person, not with ourselves. We're not defective—they are. Many people repeat the story over and over to themselves and anyone who will listen about how toxic their ex was, how they did this and that, lacked this and that, were messed up in this and that way. A belief that "it was all their fault and I was the victim, I did nothing wrong," can be just as damaging to future relationships as carrying all of the burden yourself.

These beliefs ripple into our next relationship, causing us to bring less to the table. We bring a limited and distorted version of ourselves instead of our best Self. This makes the relationship lopsided, and we end up scrambling to prove either that we have worth or that we are still the victim without power, setting ourselves up for another poor love experience that further cements our false beliefs. Without examining these beliefs, this pattern becomes a cycle that keeps us stunted and wondering if healthy love really does exist.

Relationships end because of both parties—every time. There is no relationship in which one person was to blame for the entire collapse. Even when there was abuse or infidelity, yes, the actions of one person may have been horrible and destroyed the relationship, but there were problems before the problems. Both parties contributed to the relationship dynamic based on what they brought into it from their past. Maybe one person didn't draw healthy boundaries because they didn't know how? Maybe they allowed or minimized the abuse for too long? Maybe they enabled bad behavior because of their deep-rooted need to be needed? Yes, both sides were at fault. Yes, both parties were in some ways victims and in other ways perpetrators. If they refuse to believe this, they may fall into the trap of victim mode, where they will have no chance for growth because they will not own anything. Without ownership, there is no learning and evolution. Only pointed fingers. This is one of the least favorite discussions in couples therapy when two people come in having labeled themselves as the "bad guy" and the "good guy." Is the good guy willing to own their part, even if it's a tiny part, and even if they have truly been hurt or victimized by the bad guy?

False beliefs are created for a reason. They become a self-narrative, a story that we *need* to believe about ourselves. Let's take the "I am the victim" false belief. If my ego believes that I am the victim and share no fault in my last relationship going sour, then I don't have to dig in, look at my behaviors, and take ownership of them or even of some of the unconscious patterns behind why I attract the people I do in the first place. So this "I am the victim" narrative becomes something my ego hides behind.

The crazy thing about the ego is that it believes it is easier for us to go through relationship after relationship having our hearts broken, clinging to this false belief, than it is to actually face it, own it, and do the work around dissolving it. That would require taking responsibility and ownership, and those are things the ego does not like. They feel icky and hard and disruptive to how we see ourselves. This is partly why we get into cycles, repeating similar relationship patterns over and over. And this is one of the reasons why there are so many dysfunctional relationships out there.

If we leave old relationship dances or dynamics where they died, tear up our old love blueprints, actively work through and dissolve our anger and resentment with previous partners (as well as ourselves), and earnestly attempt to dispel our false and limited beliefs formed from previous relationships (and upbringing), we can finally create something new, a brand-new love experience. Because nothing is more convincing than a new experience. And you will never give yourself one unless you start loving without your past.

John

There's usually one relationship we compare all others to, whether we are aware of it or not or willing to admit it or not. And it's not usually the healthiest relationship we've ever been in. It's the one that created the deepest imprint. For me, it was with my ex-wife. Marrying her was my jumping into the deep end. No floaties or holding the edge. All in at once. One hard bounce off the diving board without knowing anything about love or having any tools. I was in denial that I compared subsequent relationships to this one for a *very* long time. Partly because I wasn't aware I was doing it—it was unconscious—but also because I didn't want to give my ex-wife and that relationship the satisfaction of being the model. I didn't want her or that relationship to have power over me anymore.

The model would change for me many years later, after I met a therapist on a blind date, after I created new definitions of love, after I learned what a healthy relationship really looks and feels like, after therapy and tools. After loving without my past.

It didn't happen when I met Vanessa. It was a couple years in, working through my inner turbulence and resistance. I finally noticed I was comparing our relationship to previous ones, especially my marriage, but more importantly I noticed the damage it did to compare. I struggled with being present and put unfair pressure on Vanessa and the relationship to be something it wasn't. Then I asked myself, "Have I been doing this in all my other relationships?" After reviewing a quick montage of moments from previous relationships when I was comparing, checking boxes, and trying to manipulate a relationship into something rather than just focusing on creating the richest soil I could for it to grow into its own beauty, I had to conclude that, yes, of course I had.

When I realized this, I started working to consciously love without my past. What did that look like? I began to notice when I got into my head. Then I pulled myself out by practicing three things:

Curiosity.

Acceptance.

Gratitude.

I accepted Vanessa fully, for all she was. Without comparing or trying to change her. I practiced being curious about her as if I had just met her. There is power in the new. I pulled from curiosity as if we had just met, because you can't judge and be curious at the same time. Finally, I practiced gratitude for who she was, what she brought to the table (including our differences), and everything we had built so far. This is now a daily practice. Some days it's easy and some days it's hard. But it's what creates the rich soil I mentioned before.

The result? I was able to see and appreciate all the things that this new love experience had. But more importantly, I could feel it in my body. Because it's not the knowing in your head. You have to convince your body too.

My new love experience with Vanessa started to eclipse that early imprint, those early definitions. I had to drop down into my body and experience a new love in order to no longer love with my past.

Vanessa

Your past can refer to your upbringing, your parents and family dynamics, or even your friend and colleague relationships, not just your romantic relationships. All of those relationships make up the "past" that John and I are encouraging you to let go of as you try to love better in your current relationship.

Furthermore, it's important to understand that loving without your past doesn't always mean comparing what once felt good and right to what feels good and right today.

As you grow older and mature and have new life experiences, your perspective on what feels healthy should evolve as you do. The kind of relationship dynamics that felt good to you in your early twenties may not feel good to you in your late thirties. For example, friendships that centered on superficial things like shopping and money and drinking may have felt good and right to you in your early years, but those relationship dynamics don't need to be acceptable to you today.

However, what I see most often in clients who are stuck loving with their past is a confusing instinct to compare their current relationship to what they assume *shouldn't* feel good and right based on their past experiences of things not feeling good and right. For example, a consistent and reliable romantic partner may have felt boring amid the chaos of your early twenties, when you wanted to move and change jobs and cities and try new things. So now, in your midthirties, because you are stuck loving with your past, you still assume you should be with someone chaotic and dangerous, even though you desperately want someone reliable. As you can see, you can sometimes unintentionally keep yourself from the kind of relationship you want because loving with your past imposes old patterns, definitions, and dynamics that don't serve you today.

MARY AND HER TRIFECTA

Over the course of a year working with Mary, she and I realized that a trifecta of people in her life in her twenties and early thirties all triggered a very familiar feeling in her. One was a "best" friend, one was her romantic partner during that time in her life, and one was her mother. In all three relationships she never felt safe enough to express her hurts, needs, or concerns in a truthful way, and so her feelings of resentment, shame, control, judgment, and a fear of abandonment became imprinted. Whether directly or indirectly, verbally or nonverbally, it was made clear that healthy and honest communication, taking ownership, growth, and intimacy had no place in these relationships. And to be fair, Mary herself didn't have the communication tools or the emotional resilience to do so, regardless of how it would have been received by the person on the other end.

So Mary rarely, if ever, spoke up. Thus, all three relationships were emotionally lopsided, with Mary carrying the weight of silently keeping the peace and contorting herself to be someone who was always agreeable. If something hurtful was said, she would shrug it off and push it down. If a promise was broken, she would pretend it wasn't and reprimand herself for expecting the promise to be kept anyway. If a pattern of behavior made her insides churn, she would assume the responsibility for getting over it, just accepting it, rather than talking about what that behavior was bringing up in her.

These were the three most powerful relationships in Mary's life, the cornerstone of what she thought relationships should look and feel like. When we started working together, she had already done a lot of work on boundaries and understanding the dynamic between herself and her mother, she was in a fairly fresh romantic relationship, and it was starting to become apparent to her that her friendship with her "bestie" just didn't feel that great to her.

For Mary, loving without her past was coming up in the recognition that she didn't know what "good" and "right" actually looked and felt like in a relationship. Her past experiences told her that she should stay in a role that her current therapy work was helping her to challenge and outgrow. She found herself constantly bringing her past into her new relationship. Whenever her new romantic partner brought something to her that he felt was important for them to discuss, she rolled her eyes and found herself thinking, "God, do we have to talk about *everything*?!" Every time he basically forced Mary to sit in front of him and put words to something he knew was bothering her, and he didn't run, he didn't yell, and he didn't get defensive, she felt exposed. It made her feel too vulnerable. She stumbled over her words and felt stupid for not being able to express herself. Even though this was the kind of relationship she had longed for, she often wanted to end it. It was "too much." Over the course of about six months, we dissected the moments when it felt like too much, and we challenged her beliefs and her past that had convinced her that real love should look and feel unstable and unsafe and that conflict should not be talked about.

After we had wrapped up our work together, Mary emailed me that she had finally attempted to tell her best friend about an incident that hurt her feelings. The friend had gotten defensive, turned it around on her, and then totally disappeared, never speaking to her again. Mary also mentioned that while it hurt and was hard to be treated that way, she felt very secure in how she handled the situation and in the expectations she had put out there for what she wanted that relationship to look and feel like. She also said that while she still frequently found herself squirming or wanting to run every time she and her partner had difficult conversations, she was finally beginning to really enjoy the other side of those moments. Not just the feeling of closeness and depth with him that those moments usually brought, but also the feeling of pride in herself, the better understanding of her needs, and the strengthening of her voice.

Questions to Ask Yourself

What was your previous relationship dynamic? What did that dance look like from the outside? How did it feel on the inside? Are you comparing that previous dance with the one you have with your current partner? If so, what would it look like to stop and learn to dance a new dance? What dynamics have you been avoiding or trying to push against? If not partnered, can you see how this pattern has affected your past relationships?

What old love blueprints do you still hold on to? What have old relationships, or maybe your upbringing, told you about how relationships should or shouldn't look and feel? How does holding on to these blueprints—tracing them—affect your current relationship, or ones you have had in the past?

What anger and resentment do you still carry from past

relationships? What would it look like to start working on resolving and dissolving them?

What false beliefs and narratives have you formed about yourself from your previous relationships? How do these beliefs impact the relationship you're in now? If you're not in one, how did those beliefs affect your last relationship?

The Practice

The practice for this section is hard. A lot of the unraveling of old blueprints, dances, and narratives takes serious processing, and it can be extra helpful to do it with a therapist. But if you don't currently have someone you are working with on this stuff, here is how you can start the process on your own.

Take the questions you answered above one at a time. Make sure you have really sat with and thought through each of them. Don't skip through them quickly. Write out the answers.

Now take one question and for one week turn up your awareness of how you see that specific area or pattern playing out in your current relationship. If you aren't partnered, it will probably show up in your life somewhere else—with friendships, in family relationships, at work, or even just in how you talk about yourself internally. Focusing on one specific pattern at a time can help keep you from feeling overwhelmed by a lot of self work all at once, and it can help you get really familiar with how old patterns show up in the details of your life in ways you have probably been overlooking.

Repeat this practice each week, choosing another pattern to tune into. At the end of each week, write about what you have learned and experienced, as well as any revelations you have had.

Why is journaling important? All of us therapists talk about it and tell our clients to do it, but why? Language is our secondary processing tool, our primary processing tool being the felt sense of the emotion in our body. If we have a hard time accessing and making sense of that primary tool, we can use language, whether writing or speaking or a combination, to help process what otherwise might stay stuck and too hard to grasp.

CHAPTER 8

I Found Your Earring

The idea of love languages was not something we studied in grad school when we were learning to be therapists. It's not entirely science-backed. Gary Chapman didn't do extensive clinical research for his book on love languages, which is based instead on a theory he developed from his personal experiences working with clients as a Christian marriage counselor. Since its publication, that theory has exploded into mainstream relational psychology, and for good reason. While sometimes a bit broad, it is a really simple way to start looking at yourself and your partner (or kids, co-workers, family, or pretty much anyone you are close to) to see how you love each other on a daily basis. Most practicing therapists use love languages with their clients. The idea is simple, it's easy to remember and reference (we all have the book on our shelves for easy access), and it also feels very "doable." Meaning, it's not a concept that feels daunting, or even all that hard—unlike, for example, the way setting boundaries can feel for many of us.

Here is a breakdown of the five different languages, which refer to the way you feel loved, seen, and filled up in your relationships.

Words of affirmation: Specific words of encouragement, empathy, love, and acknowledgment.

Quality time: Present and connected time spent together.

Physical touch: Hugs, touching the small of the back, sitting on a lap—intimate touches.

Acts of service: Doing something for the other, whether or not they have directly asked for it. An act of service can be a gesture, like having their car washed, or it can be doing something that you notice is part of their daily routine, like making dinner.

Receiving gifts: Giving a gift, small or large, that helps the other person believe they are cherished and known.

To do a deeper dive, you can take the Love Language Quiz at the 5LoveLanguages website: www.5lovelanguages.com /quizzes/. (We suggest getting the book, *The 5 Love Languages:*

The Secret to Love that Lasts. It's a fast read and a great tool to reference.)

Really, what Chapman's love languages do is help us break down our needs in a simple and clear way that doesn't feel as vulnerable to communicate as it would if we didn't have the framework to lean on. If I can tell my partner or my parent or friend that I feel loved through acts of service, they have a reference point to return to when they are trying to show up in the relationship. If they in turn can tell me that spending quality time together makes them feel loved, I will know that I need to show up physically and be present for them. Knowing love languages takes some of the guesswork out of relationships. They can also give us a layer of accountability—for ourselves and how we need others to show up for us, but also for how we show up for others. In fact, supporting personal accountability to the other was the original intention of Chapman's theory and book.

Vanessa

I first learned about the love languages through my couples therapist when I was engaged to my ex-fiancé. I had all but begged him to see a therapist with me because, in my heart, I knew something was wrong. Our therapist tried to help us see (among many other things) that we were not feeling loved by each other and that by understanding our own and our partner's love language, we could take a nice step toward feeling more loved. I devoured the concept. My fiancé did not. I did the quiz. He did not. I discussed it in detail with our therapist. He did not. This was a pretty common pattern in our relationship. I pushed us to do more, feel more, examine more, grow more, and he just pushed back—on me. At least, that's how it always felt. Regardless, it wasn't until I was with John that I really got to practice love languages. To talk the talk. I had been giving it to my clients as homework for years, but I hadn't really experienced it myself.

Pretty early in our relationship, John and I talked love languages. I give and receive through acts of service and through touch. He gives and receives through words of affirmation and receives through touch. (Thank goodness we have that overlap!) What I was not prepared for was the realization that, while it has been incredibly helpful to know and understand each other in this way, that knowing does not in any way make it easier to feel seen and heard and appreciated by the other person. The understanding, the intellectualizing, the reading in a book—all this is only one part of how it works. One tiny *tiny* part. It's in the doing that the real work is found.

I never knew that words of affirmation are insanely hard for me to give. Not until my relationship essentially hinged on my ability to look John in the eyes and tell him, in words, *why* I loved him, what specific things I was proud of him for, or why I appreciated him. I can write the words in a card or email or text, no problem. And it's not that I can't express myself verbally—I was a communications major in undergrad, for God's sake—but being that vulnerable, live and in person, looking the other person in the eyes, makes my entire body squirm. I could go into my theory as to why

I'm like this—fear of vulnerability, fear of rejection, etc., etc.—but in regard specifically to giving words of affirmation, it doesn't actually matter. I *have* to do this thing that makes me uncomfortable or risk my partner not feeling loved by me. It's that simple.

Even this many years in, John and I go through a cycle over this issue every six months or so. John will come to me expressing that he doesn't feel desired or seen, and I have to sit on the receiving end of that and recommit to speaking up more. To giving him whatever words of affirmation I can. It can be an exhausting cycle, but one that is so important for us to stay connected and for him to feel seen and appreciated by me.

On the other side, I receive love through acts of service. When I don't get acts of service, it makes me feel resentful, used, like I am doing all the heavy lifting of everyday life and in the relationship alone. I know this stems from my codependent tendencies (we get more into this in chapter 13, "Fuck *The Giving Tree*"), but it is what it is. I can work on my codependent behaviors for the rest of my life. Meanwhile, my need for acts of service is here to stay. This means nothing to John. He does not, in any way, see how it can make me feel incredibly loved and cared for when he comes home from running errands with lunch for me. (Bonus points for just picking something he knows I'll like and not asking me what I want—decision fatigue is a real thing, y'all.) He doesn't understand how cleaning the kitchen and making me coffee in the morning makes me feel close to him and taken care of. And he sure as hell doesn't get that, more than anything, taking mundane things—household tasks and child care stuff—off my list (without my asking him) makes me feel like I am securely partnered and not alone in the mundanity of life.

At first glance, most people assume that they are doing enough to make their partner feel loved simply by showing up and being themselves. Shouldn't that be enough? I've heard this a few times as a therapist. Unfortunately, no, it isn't enough. This isn't to say that you should be trying to be someone you're not, but that if you truly love someone you need to do some work to make them feel your love. You can't simply do for them what you like done for you and assume they will hear it and feel it. The six-month cycle John and I go through, where I realize I haven't been doing enough to affirm him verbally, is an example of the trouble that can cause.

On the flip side, John is beautiful with language. He is a writer, after all. He is poetic and deep and has an ability to put things into words that doesn't come easily to me. However, while the cards and poems and small notes he leaves around the house make me smile, if I am left feeling like I'm managing the house or the child care all on my own because he's not present or he's unaware of how little he is physically doing, his words don't mean shit to me. Sorry if that sounds harsh, but it is the reality of someone who is an acts of service person.

THE EARRING

I had ten minutes before I went into four back-to-back hours of clients, and I wasn't finished drying my hair. I was running around like a chicken without a head when one of my earrings, from a pair that I love, slipped out of my fingers and into the sink drain. I screamed "FUCK!!" and stomped my feet like a child so loudly that John came running, believing I might have hurt myself. I threw a towel over the sink and told him not to run the water. When I had time later in the day, I told him, I would take the sink apart from underneath and see if I could find the earring. I muttered "Fuck! Fuck! Fuck!" all the way up the stairs as I ran to get situated for my first session. (And yes, something like this has happened sometimes right before you greet your therapist sitting calmly in their armchair, sipping tea.)

Fifty minutes later I came downstairs and saw my earring on the counter. Not only had John found my earring in that hour, but he had first gone to the hardware store to buy a wrench, then taken apart the sink, put it back together again, *and* cleaned up all of the evidence of the mess created by this project.

At that moment, I almost cried, literally. I didn't tell him that, though. I just said, "Thank you! Thank you!" and ran back to my next client session. What I did do was call pretty much everyone I knew throughout that week to recount, in detail, the story of how John found my earring. I even told the story to my therapist that week in our session. All of my female friends cooed about how he had taken charge of the situation. I talked about how it felt to not have to "handle it" alone, how I didn't have to ask for his help, how he didn't need my instruction or monitoring to make sure he was correctly taking the sink apart and putting it back together. Retrieving my earring was something that, up until that point, made me feel more loved than almost any other thing John had done for me, including the dozens of love letters and cards, the flowers, the gifts, the trips, and the back rubs. It's not that I didn't appreciate all of those other things—I did. It's just that those things don't fill me up, they don't satisfy me, they aren't my love language.

I told John days or maybe weeks later that I had talked about the earring episode with multiple people, and he was floored. Not only because he didn't see or understand why it was such a big deal to me, but also because he was confused around why I hadn't told *him* how big a deal it was to me. Why did I tell everyone else how much it made me feel loved, but not him? Why did I only give him a "thank you" but then gush about it to all of my friends? I don't know, I explained, but maybe it had something to do with feeling silly or vulnerable when expressing love and gratitude *to his face*. My eternal struggle with words of affirmation.

I missed out on a huge opportunity in that moment to make him feel as loved as he had made me feel. I didn't need to search for words, I only needed to tell him *how I felt* in the moment he had done this seemingly small thing for me, and it would have been a connection point for us. This was a huge learning experience for both of us. We realized that our love languages don't need to make sense to each other to still be valid for each of us. I also realized that I needed to stop overcomplicating words of affirmation. They don't need to be poems written in the sky. They can be simple words of appreciation in the moment for doing a nice thing.

John

Like a movie you haven't seen or plan to see but all your friends think it's great so you just recommend it to everyone anyway . . . that's what love languages were like for me. I knew about the theory, but I never really had any personal experience that made me a true believer in it. Until Vanessa.

Vanessa's main love language is acts of service, then touch, and then, of course, food. My main love language is words of affirmation, then sex all the time (shaken not stirred), and then, of course, food. Gary Chapman would argue that sex and food aren't love languages, but I would argue right back that they are. I'm kidding, but not really.

First, I may or may not be a sex addict. If I am, then I was. Meaning, I don't believe I am now. Wanting sex all the time doesn't have the grip around my neck that it used to. I couldn't breathe if I didn't have sex, all the time. I have addiction in my blood, on both branches of the family tree. I am impulsive and compulsive. I was exposed to porn and graphic images at an early age. But on a deeper level, lots of sex was my way of coping, reducing anxiety, and numbing myself so I didn't have to face feelings. It was my drug. And if I hadn't had a few spiritual cold showers in the last five years—my only explanation for why I am no longer consumed with getting laid every ten minutes—Vanessa and I would not have lasted. Yes, I'm forty-eight now and it takes more than just a stiff breeze to get it up. I also have a daughter now, so there's the whole not sleeping or having much time anymore thing. But age and having children doesn't fade addiction. So maybe I'm not a sex addict. Maybe I'm just highly sexual. I don't know. So I default to believing that something greater is transforming me. That is a choice. And it helps. It works for me.

I've put a blanket of sexual pressure on every partner I've been with. Sometimes that was a thick furry Korean blanket (dom-yo) with a dragon on it. Other times it was a light, breathable summer blanket. But either way, there was always that subtle nag in the air to be intimate with me or, more accurately, to please me. Most of my previous partners just did it because they didn't want to rock the boat. And most grew resentful, I'm sure. So this dynamic laid the tracks. Sex was what my brain associated with love. If she had sex with me, she loved me. If she didn't have sex with me, she didn't love me. And I became pouty if she didn't. A really embarrassing pouty. Like a flopping fish out of water in bed because he didn't get none pouty. I realized later it was about more than skin hunger. I felt rejected and didn't know how to express my hurt. I didn't have tools, as they say in my world. Hold that thought.

I think it started with writing little notes on the bottom of lunch bags and leaving them on her doorstep. My family had a restaurant at the time. On my break, I would drop off lunch for my girlfriend with a love note on the bottom of the bag. She was a reader. Devoured books. Loved words. So this seemed to go a long way. And of course, since we were in our twenties, hidden notes on lunch bags meant true love, right? I was showered with affection every time I did this. Like a little mouse rewarded every time he did a trick. Again, tracks were laid. But being a writer, I also loved words. And being an Aries, I like affirmation. So it was a win-win. Love notes came naturally for me. They got me the most bang for my buck. Showing and receiving love through words of affirmation became the norm in all my relationships thereafter. Until I met Vanessa.

I didn't get the reward (praise) I did in previous relationships when I gave Vanessa words. She appreciated them. But they didn't land the same. If I wrote her name in the sky, she would wonder how much it cost. But if I washed her car or retrieved an earring stuck in the drain, she would throw her arms around me like she had lost me and found me. This was all new to me. It was like being with someone who spoke Russian when I only spoke Chinese, and I struggled with it. I thought maybe we weren't compatible. Add to this our different sexual appetites and I felt disconnected and rejected *often*. Until I started to understand the concept of love languages, how they impact relationships, and what to do about it.

The earring incident was a huge revelation. After hearing that she told all her friends about how I got the earring out of the sink drain—which I didn't think was a big deal at all—I realized just what acts of service meant to her. In a nutshell, everything. Her definition of love is to make someone's life a little easier. Because it means you're not just thinking about the person but you're also doing something about it. This love language was also tied to her story. Being the eldest sibling who took care of everyone else for most of her life, it was refreshing for her to be taken care of for once. That felt like love to her. And it was fair.

Today I fully accept our different ways of giving and receiving love. I understand that we are different people, and I no longer try to change that. I have zero interest in trying to convince Vanessa to eat meat. So why should I try to change her love preferences? It's who she is and to love her means to accept and embrace that. She has also accepted the way I give and receive love. With acceptance comes the letting go of attempts to change or control the other person. It also releases expectations, a huge cliff we fall off when they're not met. Asking someone to love the way you love is not a fair expectation. It's a trap, and it punctures the relationship.

With the foundation of acceptance and the release of expectations based on our own definitions, we can now try to meet each other's needs. Not because we are pressured to or forced to, but because we want to. This dissolves resentment and keeps the love magnets facing each other. And this is what swimming past the breakers looks like.

Instead of just focusing on how I want to be loved and being hurt and disappointed if I am not loved that way, I now consider how Vanessa wants to be loved. And I ask myself if I am loving her that way. Chances are I'm not. So I try to speak her love language. As a practice. Some days it's easy. Some days it's hard. But the attempt is what matters. Because it comes back. She notices and hits the ball back. Then you have two people considering the way each other wants to be loved. This is where relationship glue is produced instead of drift. Without this process, you're just two people trying to change each other. And that never works.

Questions to Ask Yourself

First, take the online love languages quiz if you haven't already and have your partner do the same. Now that both of you know what your primary and secondary love languages are, ask yourself if your love tank is full or not. If it's not full, ask yourself how it could be fuller. Where and in what ways can you ask your partner for more of what you need? Remember, having your love tank filled isn't 100 percent on your partner; you have to speak up and ask for it too.

Now flip this question. Based on your partner's language, where can you step up your game and show them more love in their preferred way? An extra credit question is to ask if and why it feels uncomfortable for you to give or receive in the language of your partner, and then to share that self-inquiry with them.

The Practice

Love languages are really just a CliffsNotes version of emotional needs. They help us understand what makes us feel loved and seen and how to communicate that in a simple way to our partner. Look at the languages as a primer for going deeper into other needs you have in your relationship. Also, needs don't always have to "make sense," and they can change as you grow. Many of us don't communicate our needs to our partner because we feel like we will look silly, weak, or needy. This is simply untrue. All humans have needs, and not communicating them to the other person sets us and them up for failure 100 percent of the time.

For many of us, tuning into our uncommunicated and thus unmet needs involves first remembering times when we felt safe, loved, understood, held, heard, free, appreciated, respected, or honored. Then we can identify the need that was fulfilled in those moments. What did the other person (partner or not) do or say that led us to feel that amazing way? When you do this, sit with the memory of the *feeling*. Now, if you could re-create that in your day-to-day, what might it look like?

Our needs don't always have to be met through grand gestures (look at the earring example), and sometimes we have the means and responsibility to take care of them ourselves. Once you have identified a few of your needs, communicate them to your partner. (This is sometimes the hardest part.) Ask them to help you feel more X by doing more Y, and then let them know how they are doing along the way. Take out the guesswork. Guesswork in relationships only leads to unmet expectations and resentment.

CHAPTER 9

That's Not What I'm Saying!

We all know how important communication is. The ability to communicate in a healthy way is the protein of every relationship. Without it, you just have a lot of carbs you can't break down. Or fat. The relationship will not grow stronger. But most of us are not good at communication. Because no one teaches us. Because it's a muscle we don't exercise. Because expressing our feelings in a healthy way does not come naturally. What *does* come naturally is reacting from our emotions and talking over each other. What *does* come naturally is our learned behavior from our parents, who slammed doors or gave each other (or us) the silent treatment. What *does* come naturally is constantly blaming the other person and holding resentment from not feeling understood instead of taking the initiative to learn how to communicate better.

At this very moment, in couples therapy offices around the world, I would bet there are hundreds if not thousands of couples diagnosing their relationship as having "communication problems." Communication is a broad and gaping hole of a term that we throw many of our relationship dysfunctions into. In fact, "trouble communicating" is often what lands a couple across from us in therapy. But what does "communication" actually mean? What's at the root of communication issues?

John

I'll be honest, I have never in my life taken a communications class. If it wasn't for my therapist training, I would not have any tools for communicating in a healthy way. Like most people, I would have only learned from mistakes, trial and error, and many hurtful fights and sleepless nights. And even then, wanting to learn how to communicate better becomes one of those things that falls to the wayside, right next to meditation and fixing that chipping paint in the corner of the shower ceiling that bothers the shit out of you and will only take thirty minutes to fix but never gets done. It's not until we are five sessions deep in couples counseling that we realize communication is a craft, an art. It requires education, effort, and practice. We had no idea. But even after that realization, our dedication to learning how to communicate better is usually short-lived.

I think maybe we should have communication tattoo marks on our arms to indicate, like karate belts, who has actually done the work and who hasn't. Who can provide a safe space and who can't. So we know going into a relationship what to expect. If we could literally see how good or bad someone is at communicating, like we can see abs and biceps, the world would be a safer place. No joke.

FAST ELBOWS

Okay, let's get to it. The topic of communication is vague and vast. There are so many angles and ways into the "how" of it. And we aren't going to solve all of your communication issues in just one chapter of this one book. A good way to approach it is like Olympic weightlifting.

Weightlifting is precision based. One small tweak in movement can affect the entire lift. So if you give an athlete too many instructions, she will do nothing. You have to give her one specific note at a time. For example, "fast elbows." That's when you solely focus on whipping your elbows under the bar as fast as you can to catch a power clean. If she focuses on this one instruction, executing it will most likely align her feet and her hips and correct other parts of her movement naturally. If you instead give her multiple instructions, like "move your feet wider," "have fast elbows," "pull sooner," and "look straight ahead," she will most likely do none of these things. It's too much to take in at one time. It's overwhelming. Learning how to communicate better is the same. Results come faster by focusing on a few things rather than trying to do or change too many at once.

Here are our three "fast elbows" notes for communication. These are the instructions that we feel have helped not only our clients but also our own relationship. We believe that if you focus on these three notes, things will start to align. You will be a better communicator, and your relationship will have more protein, the building blocks for growth.

1. TRY TO UNDERSTAND BEFORE TRYING TO BE UNDERSTOOD, I.E., TRYING TO CREATE SAFETY.

JOHN

For most of my life, I would think of a comeback while my girlfriend was talking. It was like we were in a courtroom and I was a young hotshot lawyer trying to prove my case. I couldn't listen to her because I was too busy thinking of a defense. It took a divorce, a master's degree in psychology, and 3,000 face-to-face hours as an intern providing people with therapy to realize that good communication all starts with safety. If you're trying to prove something or to express yourself before really listening to your partner, you are not creating a safe space. If, as I used to do (and still sometimes do), you interrupt your partner and think of a reply, an angle, a defense before fully understanding their position, perspective, and heart, there is no soil for communication. It's like trying to grow vegetables in cement.

This pattern is so ingrained in me that I still struggle with it today. When Vanessa sits me down to talk about something that's been on her mind, I feel my body tense, like it's preparing itself for a fight. I instinctively grab my shield and sword. But then I think about having "fast elbows" and focus on trying to understand before trying to be understood. I don't ignore how I feel in my body. I just become aware of it and know that that feeling comes from growing up in a loud Korean family where people spoke at and over each other instead of listening and understanding first.

If you also grew up in a family that yelled at each other and ignored feelings, your body has also been conditioned to believe this is the norm. Or maybe your conditioned norm was formed by growing up in a family where people withdrew when they were upset, became silently angry, and then swallowed it all, swept it under the rug, and pretended like everything was fine. You would also have a metaphorical shield and sword you instinctively pick up to defend yourself when you feel a potential threat, conflict, or tension. The same thing happens if you grew up fighting for food with your siblings. Chances are, you will not be a food sharer at dinner parties as an adult. You will protect what's on your plate and your friends will think you're weird. But you're not weird. Food just activates survival mode in you.

So hard conversations can put us in our survival mode—the kid fighting to be heard. We either fight and scream to be heard or we shut down and don't even try, depending on the patterns we saw when we were younger. The ways in which we communicate or don't communicate are tracks that were laid from birth.

Knowing this, I remind myself that I am reconditioning my body to not panic when confronted. To create and explore a new space by breathing through the tug of the old—the need to be understood before understanding. While learning to sit and grow in the new—the trying to understand first. I know that, like building muscle at the gym, it's going to take lots of reps. So I try to be patient with myself and see each sit-down (talk) as an exercise to become a stronger communicator.

VANESSA

I have a BA in communications. I barely remember anything that I was taught. I spent a lot of money to go to a private university to learn to live on my own, to party (a lot), and to get some great internships that ultimately led to my first career in marketing. But the day-to-day classes? I have a memory of, like, two (shout-out to Susan Picillo for being my only memorable professor). This is all to let you know that communication in a relationship is not only hard but also something you can't do or get better at by reading and taking classes. If it were, I would be a master at it (or at least, a bachelor?).

You get better at communicating through trial by fire. You put yourself out there, you stumble, you look stupid, you mess up, you try again. And little by little, you learn new skills. It's like riding a bike. You train your nervous system to not react in the same way it was trained as a child. For example, I grew up in a very defensive household. You did not admit when you were wrong, you did not sit and listen to the other person without talking over and at them about your position, you scoffed and rolled your eyes at vulnerable emotions, and you sure as hell didn't apologize. So it is no surprise that trying to understand before being understood was, and still is, a very foreign concept to me.

I have been actively working on improving my ability

to sit and listen, without interrupting, probably only since entering grad school to become a therapist, and I was in my thirties when I went back to school. For me, arguing immediately brings up two reactions:

1. The relationship isn't working! Abort! Abort! And/or:

2. I did something wrong, so I am bad.

It took a lot of reflection—and a partner (John) who is able to observe and reflect softly back to me the reactions he notices in me—to realize that any conversation about us, about something I said or did that hurt his feelings, or about something that we need to work on in the relationship, triggers deep shame in me. It brings up a feeling of not being good enough, of not trying hard enough, of failing, of being bad. And when the shame creeps in, I bow out. Meaning, I basically dissociate. I leave my body and go into my head, where I am formulating the why and the how of leaving the relationship. (We will dive into attachment styles later—you might already be able to tell I lean a bit avoidant.)

This understanding of myself has given me a huge amount of self-compassion, and it has also given me opportunities to try to give myself new experiences. When John and I have a heated conversation or argument and I feel my defenses kicking in, I start to repeat "Try to understand before being understood" in my head over and over. It has become a mantra of mine. I also sit in my seat and do something to stay in my body, like pinching my leg or digging my nails into the chair, and then I repeat the mantra over and over again. This practice forces me to stay present, in my body, and out of my head. It keeps my fight-or-flight response from taking hold of my brain entirely, so that I hopefully can maintain enough logical brain functioning to be less reactive in my responses. It helps me to avoid jumping to defend myself or talking over John and instead to give him the space to be heard.

"Try to understand before being understood" has honestly been a game-changer for me and my relationship communication. Plus, this one instruction lays the soil for the second "fast elbows," as John calls it—reading subtext.

2. READ SUBTEXT.

There are two levels of communication: content and subtext. Content is what's literally being said. "I don't care if he's just a friend, I don't want you to see him anymore." Subtext is what the person is really saying: "I feel threatened by your friendship and I struggle with trust." Content is information. Subtext is what's running underneath.

Most of us just focus on the content, not the subtext. Chew on this. Only 3 percent of communication is content; 97 percent is subtext, tone, and body language. So if you're only focused on the words coming out of your partner's mouth, you only understand 3 percent of what they are saying. This is one of the greatest mistakes when it comes to communication, and a major reason why people feel unheard.

It's imperative that we understand what is happening underneath. Communication is not about the words. Words are just skin. It's like acting. You cannot be a good actor if you don't have the ability to read between the lines. You won't know and then be able to express what the character truly wants and feels. What people say sometimes doesn't line up with how they actually feel. Therefore, you cannot be a great communicator if you can't read what your partner is saying underneath the words. Truth lives in the subtext. Not on the surface.

It's also not your job to play detective in order to dig down until you find the subtext. We are only responsible for keeping our own side of the street clean (an AA slogan). Meaning, each of us is responsible in any relationship only for being clear and kind in our communication and for trying to create an open and empathetic space so that the other person feels safe enough to explore and communicate what's really going on for them, underneath the content. If your partner isn't picking up on the subtext underneath your words, it isn't necessarily their fault.

JOHN

I've always been a literal person. "You didn't say it, so how was I supposed to know?" That was my go-to defense. It's not me. It's you. "*You* didn't say it. So you need to work on being able to say things. I'm not a mind reader." This wasn't me hitting the ball back. It was me leaving the game.

Yes, no one can read minds. But we can all read body language, tone, energy. We can read between the lines and pick up on what is *not* being said. Or at least we can try to. And that's what's important. The attempt. Because you only get better the more you try. By knowing our partner's story and what they struggle with, we can put two and two together and have an idea of what they might be trying to say. Or not say. None of this is literal, but it's all part of communication. You are not listening for words. You are instead reading the whole person, considering who they are and how they are because of their story. And the more you know that person, the less you can use the excuse "But you didn't say anything."

For example, I know when we're trying to all get out of the house to go somewhere and Vanessa is gathering Logan's diaper bag, milk, toys, bib, etc., and she's running around talking to herself, my job is to ask her if there's anything I can do. She may say, "No, I'm good," or "Yes, can you get me. . . ." But either way, just the fact that I asked her if she needed anything brings her calm. Her energy changes almost instantly because I addressed the subtext. What she's saying underneath is, can you ask to help me to show that you see me struggling right now? Asking for help is hard for her. It doesn't come naturally. So sometimes I have to read her energy and body language to hear what she's really saying or asking. And if I address that, she feels more heard and loved.

Today I struggle with the complete opposite. After mostly being in relationships with women who had difficulty expressing themselves, I now focus so much on reading subtext that I dismiss what is actually being said. When I ask Vanessa if something's wrong and she says "No, nothing's wrong," I assume she's lying. I assume she's hiding something because she struggles with expressing her feelings. Now I'm playing shit out in my head for the rest of the day and creating scenarios that are not true. By the time I get back home, I am coming in loaded and hot. In my head, we have already broken up and gotten back together five times. And then broken up again.

I have been trained to always look deeper, but sometimes there is nothing deeper than what is said. My work to be a better communicator in my relationship currently is to swing back and know when to just listen to what is being said and accept that as truth.

VANESSA

In grad school we called this "content versus process." We were trained to listen through the content, to interrupt it and get to the process. Content can be a way to hide. It can keep us in our head, thinking, recounting, explaining details rather than living in the feelings and the memories or associations that emotions can bring up. Feeling and emotion are hard for many of us, making us vulnerable, and so we stay in our heads and hide behind content. In our day-to-day lives this is usually fine. But in our intimate relationships and conversations, staying in our heads is a wall, for both the person talking and the person listening.

Communicating and listening for the process, the subtext, is beneficial to both parties. As the speaker, if I can work on slowing myself down and realize that I am talking, talking, talking, and not feeling, I can go deeper and communicate to John what I am feeling, what I am struggling with, what

I am needing. It becomes less about "I am *so* sick of picking up the dirty socks you leave all over the house," and more about "constantly picking up your socks makes me feel like you don't respect my time and you expect me to do all the work around the house. It's important to me that I feel respected in this relationship, and not leaving your socks all over the house will help me feel that way." These are two very different conversations.

As someone who struggles to speak up, I know it is important to remember that it is not the job of the listener to constantly be trying to see and hear what's underneath the content of what I say. That can be exhausting. And if the listener is too good at discerning the subtext, sometimes the other person can get away with not speaking up and communicating their needs. Still, it can be helpful if the listener reflects back what they are hearing in an empathetic way and asks feeling-related questions. This practice can help the other person slow down and tap into their process. For example:

Speaker: I am *so* sick of picking up the dirty socks you leave all over the house!

Listener: I hear you saying you are frustrated with me, and I imagine you also feel overwhelmed. Is that right?

Speaker: Yes, thank you, that is right. It's just that constantly picking up your socks makes me feel like you don't respect my time and you expect me to do all the work around the house. It's important to me that I feel respected in this relationship, and not leaving your socks all over the house will help me feel that way.

Sometimes it's hard to get to that last part without the listener reflecting back what they hear. If the listener gets defensive and takes the speaker's content personally, neither of them can invite in the feeling and slow down the conversation.

John and I have come to the conclusion that sometimes communicating needs is a two-way street. If you know your partner well, and you know they struggle with, say, feeling like they are "in it alone" or that they always have to "do everything," then you'll want to be more sensitive to that. In training yourself to be more aware of subtext, you are helping your partner write a new narrative. You help them feel seen and understood if they don't have to communicate the same need over and over again, because occasionally you anticipate it based on your understanding of them and their story. And the benefit of being aware of subtext with our partners is that it helps us not take what they are saying to us personally. So if I lose my communication skills in a moment of overwhelm and come in hot with "I am so sick of picking up your socks!," John, listening for subtext, can remember that this isn't about him. It's actually about me and my story.

3. HEALTHY COMMUNICATION FALLS SOMEWHERE BETWEEN VERBALLY VOMITING AND SWEEPING IT UNDER THE RUG.

JOHN

I used to believe that love and communication meant telling your partner everything, hiding nothing. That was what doing life with your partner should look like. You should be completely transparent. Love like plastic wrap, not aluminum foil. Nothing should be hidden. Nothing. If you were hiding something, then you yourself were hiding. But after many expired relationships and therapy sessions, I've learned that plastic wrap suffocates people and it's *not* what healthy love and communication look like. Telling all and hiding nothing is a distorted idea about communication I've absorbed from my alcoholic father, who wore his emotions on both sleeves. There is responsibility in disclosure. You can't just verbally vomit on people. That's what children do. And that's what I *used* to do.

The first crowbar that cracked my marriage years ago was when I confessed to her that I had gotten a few erotic massages when I was in my midtwenties because I thought I was going to marry my then girlfriend and I hadn't had many sexual experiences. I felt God telling me I needed to confess my sins. Looking back, I don't know if it was God or my guilty conscience. Or maybe it was a shame-lined secret I didn't want to carry anymore. But it weighed on me. So I told my wife.

It did not go over well. At all. All she heard was that I had cheated on my ex-girlfriend. She didn't understand the part about me being a horny twenty-something or see that getting a few happy endings to get things out of my system had been a ridiculous idea. Anyway, it was something she didn't have to know. It's something I did before I even knew her. I didn't have to disclose this part of my story. But at the time I thought that love meant you disclosed *everything*. That your partner should know every detail about you, past, present, and future. I was wrong. And irresponsible. There are some things your partner doesn't have to know. My wife never looked at me the same after that confession.

VANESSA

Almost everything we do in relationships, including communication, can be taken to one of two extremes. One extreme is what John is referring to: "word vomit," i.e., overcommunicating. The other extreme is not communicating at all. I tend toward this side of the spectrum. I am a great talker. I can talk to a brick wall (and the conversation will be riveting, I assure you). I'm also a great communicator at work. I can work through problems and clearly articulate needs and potential solutions. But throw me into something vulnerable and I am a master at sweeping it all under the rug in order to not rock the boat.

In the beginning, I remember saying to John, "We don't need to talk about *everything*." And he also used to constantly ask me what was wrong, because he sensed (and was usually correct) that I wasn't speaking up about something. His spidey senses developed in his previous relationships were helping him here. I would usually say "nothing" even if there was something. That's not fair, to either party. I wasn't allowing him to grow and trust the relationship, and I wasn't pushing myself to grow by practicing speaking up. I was annoyed when he would ask me if everything was okay, but how could I have expected him to not constantly be digging and trying to share and communicate *everything* when he was always sensing that I wasn't honestly communicating the important stuff? That's crazy-making.

Through practice we can figure out what the communication middle ground is. The point between the two extremes. It does not come naturally for me to speak up. Avoiding conflict, not being clear and direct about my upsets or needs, downplaying what I'm feeling as not being worth speaking up over, feeling needy for having needs—these are my default behaviors, based on false beliefs, that have become the basis for my communication strategies. Not surprisingly, they do not work. Period. I have had enough relationships (both romantic and friend) end partly because of my inability to communicate to know that my way is most certainly not the right way.

Let's ask ourselves some hard questions to see how we can work to find the middle ground between our extremes—what John and I call "responsible communication."

Questions to Ask Yourself

Are you someone who tends to share easily (maybe a little too easily) what's going through your mind? If so, try asking yourself what you might need to take responsibility for. What is yours to investigate, to own, to sit with and not place on your relationship? Are you using your partner to soothe your own anxiety rather than to build the skills to self-soothe? What is your hope in sharing the things you share? To change the other person? To be understood and accepted fully? To offload some of your heavy or anxious feelings onto the other person so you can feel a little better yourself?

Or are you someone who struggles to communicate? If so, start by asking yourself why you shut down or make a decision not to share. What are you afraid of? Be honest with yourself. Why do you feel like you can't trust the other person with your true feelings? Are you choosing to stay in a relationship lined with resentment, one in which you're not heard or seen, rather than risk an upset or being left by your partner? Does that feel fulfilling to you? Are you resentful at all?

The Practice

TRYING TO UNDERSTAND BEFORE TRYING TO BE UNDERSTOOD

First, set the intention to try to understand your partner (or friend, or co-worker, or family member) first. Most likely, doing this is not your default. Like many of us, you may interrupt with "yeah but" and argue or defend yourself while the other person is still talking. Or you may not be saying anything yet, but in your head you're preparing your comeback. Or both. Set the intention to *try* to understand what the other person is saying first. Then take a breath. Wait until they are completely finished. Don't interrupt. Finally, repeat back what you heard them saying. This is a practice that helps the other person feel seen, heard, and understood, and it is also a way for you to focus more on what they are saying because you have to listen closely enough to be able to repeat what they have said.

READING SUBTEXT

The practice here, as with trying to understand before be-ing understood, is to repeat back what you think you are hearing the other person say, but going a step further by saying something like "I can imagine that makes you feel (resentful, unseen, underappreciated, alone, etc)." If mak-ing a suggestion like this feels a little too dangerous in the beginning of this practice, you can also ask the other person to put words to what they're feeling. When they say some-thing biting, hurtful, or loaded, you can ask them directly what they are really trying to say. Try saying something like "It sounds like there is a really strong feeling attached to what you just said, and I would like to hear what it is." Or, "It sounds like you might be hurt about something, and I would really like to understand."

VERBAL VOMITING VERSUS SWEEPING IT UNDER THE RUG

If you are the verbal vomiter, consider how your expres-sion will affect the other person before you share. What is the purpose or intention of your disclosure? Are you sharing more for you or for them? Do you want them to hold something that doesn't belong to them because it will make you feel better in the short term? Do you want to hurt them because you are hurting? Your practice is about getting really honest with yourself around your motives for communicating.

If you are the one who tends to not speak up, then your practice here is to do the opposite. To overcommunicate. Talk about every little annoyance or prickly feeling that comes up. And since that will feel very uncomfortable and even a little over the top, you can even let the other person know ahead of time that it is something you are working on and practicing. So they can expect it, let them know that your overcommunicating is your way of trying to course-correct. The funny thing is, what you feel is overcommunicating probably won't actually feel that way to them. It will probably just seem like you are finally speaking up.

CHAPTER 10

Cut and Run: Understanding Attachment Styles

When the going got tough, his instinct was to want less of me. Mine was to want more of him. That black hole in between crushed us.

—BUDDY WAKEFIELD

HOW MANY ROUNDS IS TOO MANY?

The intake call was only with Sonya, not with Peter too. She was recounting the fight they had had two days prior that ended in her brandishing a knife at him and ultimately kicking in a door. Which had led Peter to say, "We either talk to someone or we're done."

And then there was that time when Peter tried to leave while they were fighting and Sonya threw herself on top of his car and wouldn't let go. Screaming so loud that the neighbors called the cops.

And then there was that time during a fight when he had told her he was done, he couldn't handle this anymore, and her response was to lock herself in the bedroom with a knife and threaten suicide.

And then there was that time, and then there was that time, and then . . .

There were so many concerns in their relationship, but in my professional opinion, one of the most glaring was how extreme their behavior became when their attachment styles were activated, especially hers, and how the relationship had become essentially unsafe for both of them. Sonya was incredibly anxiously attached and Peter was incredibly avoidant. The two opposite sides of the spectrum.

What does that mean exactly? Well, whenever there was conflict—which there often was—Peter wanted to run, and he said as much, both verbally and nonverbally. His desire to run then made Sonya fly off the handle in an emotional, anxious panic. For this reason, in the beginning they were almost completely incapable of having any hard conversation without it turning into World War III.

We worked for months on communication skills, empathy building, and each owning their part and getting in touch with the intense emotional activations that were happening in the midst of the upset. They separated and came back together three times within the eighteen months we worked together. It was a relationship that made even me, the therapist, think multiple times (and even verbalize a couple of times), "*Why* are you two together? Are you *sure* this is the relationship you want?" It was exasperating, to say the least. But they kept showing up, committed to learning and growing as much as they could. There seemed to be a deep understanding that even if therapy didn't save their relationship, this type of behavior would haunt them in the next one, and the next one after that, and so it needed to be sorted out *now*.

The way their activated attachment styles manifested in their behavior was extreme, but it perfectly illustrates one of the key points to take away from this chapter even if Sonya and Peter's relationship doesn't totally remind you of your own current or past relationship: Avoidants activate the anxious, who activate avoidants. These two attachment styles *love* each other. It's an example of two very different personality types being unconsciously drawn to each other because of what they say they hate the most—their emotional responses.

The psychologists John Bowlby and Mary Ainsworth identified four attachment styles in their original research. The basic gist of attachment theory is that we develop our attachment styles in childhood based on our caregiver's responses to our emotional needs for connection and safety. The research is actually still growing. More recent research discusses attachment styles as more of a spectrum than a fixed set of four, and it has shown that your style can change based on the type of relationship and person you are relating to. The research has also expanded to take some of the blame off of our parents. They may set the stage, but our attachment styles are formed through many relational experiences (and are continually developing throughout our lives).

Attachment theory is nuanced, like humans are. But at the basic level there is a spectrum that runs from "fearful avoidant" to "avoidant" to "anxious," with "secure" landing somewhere in the middle of those three. Although it is a spectrum of four styles, common parlance refers to only three: anxious, avoidant, and secure.

The anxious person struggles with the relationship taking over their life and typically becomes overly fixated on the other person—what they are doing, what their body language is communicating, what they might be thinking, etc. This person may struggle with boundaries and wonder constantly if their partner still wants them. They need constant validation and reassurance from their partner, and their feelings of self-worth are tied to the relationship.

The avoidant struggles with intimacy and expressing feelings, thoughts, and emotions. They are often accused of being distant and closed off. They flood or get overwhelmed by feelings easily. The closer someone gets and the needier they seem to become, the more an avoidant withdraws.

Those who are securely attached appreciate their own self-worth and ability to be themselves in intimate relationships. They openly seek support and comfort from their partner. They are similarly happy when their partner relies on them for emotional support. They are able to maintain

emotional balance and seek healthy ways to manage conflict in their relationships.

Some of the research also tells us that people are "only
as needy as their unmet needs," as Amir Levine and Rachel
Heller put it in their book *Attached*. What they mean is that
when our emotional needs are being met, we can all function from a more securely attached place. This is sometimes
referred to as the "dependency paradox." It is important
that we understand that as humans we are dependent on
other people to an extent. It's about a certain level of self-
understanding (isn't it all?) and an ability to communicate
a need without spiraling uncontrollably into the unhealthy
behavior patterns of clinging or pushing away. And when it
comes to romantic relationships, it's about finding and fos-
tering a connection with an equally self-aware partner who
shows a commitment to understanding you as much as themselves and a desire to continue to learn and grow together.

Vanessa

"When you said that thing earlier in front of Pat, it really
hurt my feelings. It felt like you were mothering me and
being condescending and talking down to me."

In this moment my face gets hot, I swallow hard, and
I immediately find myself leaving my body. My thoughts
become a swirling mass of wanting to end the relationship
("Fuck him," "This is why you should leave," "I'm so over
this shit") and shame ("I can't believe I did that," "This is
why people think I'm a bitch," "This is why all my relationships end").

Attachment styles—currently one of the hot pop psychology topics. Everyone wants to know their attachment style, their partner's and friends' attachment styles. They want to know the why, the how, and they want answers to the two biggest questions of all: How do I become more secure? And how do I find a partner who is secure?

John and I went to different grad schools to become therapists but agree that in both programs we only brushed over the idea of attachment styles when studying Bowlby and Ainsworth. That gave us only a bird's-eye view of the theory. It was not until we became working therapists and saw how misunderstood and unmanaged attachment styles were such a glaringly obvious issue in so many of our clients' relationships that we really did a deep dive. And then there was us. We noticed that our different attachment styles were a major rub in the relationship pretty early on. John tends to lean more anxious, while my style is avoidant.

This difference manifests in our behavior in many ways. From my (clearly avoidant) perspective, in disagreements or fights I get flooded, want to shut down and walk away, while John wants to sit and talk it out (sometimes to death). He wants to be connected, all the time, and I like to be connected sometimes and then have my personal and emotional space the rest of the time. When things are feeling off or there is some sort of disconnect between us, he clings and I distance. I tend to keep things inside and have a hard time expressing myself and my needs clearly. John tends to express *everything*. If I'm not giving him enough emotional attention, he gets very moody, whereas I could probably get by on emotional scraps for far too long.

Obviously, John perceives these moments differently. But from my perspective, as someone who leans more avoidant, when I feel emotionally activated I shut down, withdraw, put up a wall and protect myself. I am hypersensitive to feeling like my independence is being taken away or questioned in any way, and I have a hard time with sustained intimate connection. It can feel draining and bring up intense resentment and a desire to be alone.

The hopeful thing about attachment styles is that we can become more and more securely attached as we experience healthy attachment in our adult relationships. So as I, the avoidant, am shown that my partner can be firm and clear about their need for connection and can also respect my autonomy and not take it personally when I need some space, I can begin to trust that I won't be suffocated and can then connect more consistently. As I experience being with someone who communicates clearly and expects me to do the same, and who can respect when I am feeling emotionally overwhelmed and need a break, I can soften into the safety and respect of the relationship more. Because I'm aware of my tendency to be avoidant, being given *both* the space and the loving boundaries of how John expects me to treat him and show up in our relationship allows me to lower my walls. I am able to reflect on my emotional responses and see that they are mostly a knee-jerk reaction I've adopted for protection. Then I can challenge myself to choose differently based on the kind of connection I truly want.

John

I didn't realize I had an anxious attachment style until I met Vanessa. I thought I was secure as fuck. I mean I studied this shit. I don't lose myself in anyone. I find myself! Usually the neediness and wanting reassurance comes from whoever I'm with, not from me. But then again, I never loved a true avoidant. Someone who also spoke a different love language than me. That can flip the magnet for sure.

My previous partners may have had avoidant tendencies (not all of them, of course), like not being able to express feelings or hold eye contact in the bedroom. But everyone I have loved connected on how we gave and received love. That was the bridge. Love notes. Thoughtful cards. Gushy feelings on paper. The love blanket we shared. With Vanessa, I was in my own sleeping bag. But we were in the same tent, and I trusted that. Because that tent had two master's degrees on the wall. But as it turns out, having letters after your name doesn't mean shit when it comes to relationships.

After the first year of being with Vanessa, I felt myself needing more. I needed reassurance. I needed her to tell me I was sexy. I needed her to desire me and express it with her legs wrapped around me when I walked in the front door. Things I have gotten from previous exes. Okay, maybe not the wrapped legs. But definitely compliments and dirty talk like college kids doing long distance for the first time.

And the more I needed this and expressed it, the more Vanessa probably wanted to run. My anxious attachment style was triggering her avoidant style. Of course, my first reaction was to blame and get her to change the way she loved me. I wouldn't be so needy if she'd just write my name in the sky once in a while and say that she wanted to go underneath the desk while I was doing a Zoom session. (Don't worry, just a fantasy. It never happened.) But that wasn't how Vanessa was wired. Instead, she expressed her own needs and *that's* how I knew I was still anxiously attached. I saw it in how hard it was for me to give her the space she wanted and needed to feel safe, to be able to let her guard down, which would then allow her to give me more of what I wanted. It's not that she didn't love me or find me attractive. She needed to not have to protect her autonomy—what she was used to. By not creating a safe space and instead always asking for things, I was making it harder for her to get out of protection mode. Once I had this revelation, I changed my tune. I focused more on creating that safe space and less on asking for things.

Finally I was able to let go of her leg and hold her hand. I started to think about all Vanessa's previous relationships and how her partners could not do that for her. Those experiences are partly why she is an avoidant. No one had provided a safe space long enough for her to feel at ease and loved. Now I had motivation. I wanted to be the first one who gave her that. Yes, part ego. But also because I suddenly had empathy for her. Being avoidant wasn't her fault. She didn't have the backing. I imagined her as a little girl who wasn't "lovey-dovey" enough and was doing her best to protect herself. This wasn't about love. This was about learning to touch the stove again, even when you know it's not on. This was about fear.

With my dial turned to empathy, I started to make an effort to understand her needs more instead of trying to get her to understand mine, to create a safe space that wasn't lined with shoulds. I not only accepted how she loved me but started to appreciate it. For the first time. It's funny that when you stop focusing on your own needs and wants, you can see what the other person is bringing to the table in a way you couldn't before. Vanessa was giving me so many things I had not experienced in previous relationships. Really good things. She was aware of herself and took ownership. I could talk to her about anything. She wasn't defensive. And if she was, she acknowledged it. She took care of herself. She was thoughtful. She enjoyed our sexy time. Basically, Vanessa was the healthiest, most present person I'd ever been with. And all I could focus on was the fact that she probably wouldn't go down on me while I was doing a session (a fantasy of mine, but nothing I would ever actually do, don't worry). That's when I realized it was me. Not her.

Avoidants activate the anxious. And vice versa. If you're anxious and your partner is being avoidant, that makes you more anxious. And if you're an avoidant and your partner is being anxious, that just makes you more avoidant. And yet avoidants and the anxious are generally drawn to each other. This is what's tricky. What we're drawn to is also what activates us. Therefore, both the avoidant and the anxious must be aware that they activate each other. Instead of blaming and trying to change the other, they need to choose to lean into their discomfort, into what they are not used to. This is difficult to do. It's not like brushing your teeth with the opposite hand. Leaning into what feels uncomfortable goes against our wiring and the way we have been maneuvering in relationships our entire life. But it's what flips that magnet back. It's where you can stretch and grow. It's what can get both the avoidant and the anxious to finally start swimming toward a secure attachment and healing wounds from the past. That's the beauty of difficult relationships. They can heal us. The burden of being with someone with a different attachment style can also be the greatest gift.

Questions to Ask Yourself

If you haven't researched your attachment style yet, a good book to begin with is *Attached* by Amir Levine and Rachel S. F. Heller. It's a bit oversimplified, but it will get you started. As we mentioned, attachment styles are very nuanced, so don't place yourself in an all-or-nothing box. But it is helpful to have a sense of where you tend to land on the spectrum.

Now, once you have some good background info, start to question your emotional responses. Attachment styles tend to get activated when we feel threatened by potential rejection, abandonment, or engulfment. Does your response to intense emotional activation tend to fall more on the avoidant side or the anxious side? Do you notice your responses being different depending on the type of relationship? Do you see those responses changing based on how the other person responds to *your* response?

If you haven't yet, discuss your attachment style with your partner and your therapist if you have one. They can help you turn the mirror around to see how certain behaviors might actually be coming from an activated attachment style. This stuff can be hard for us to see in ourselves at first.

Exploring your attachment style is not just about your behaviors, but also about the thoughts and beliefs that usually perpetuate them. For example, if you pull from a more anxious place, you might find yourself thinking that the person you're with is the *only* person in the world who will ever love you, and so you have to cling tight, make this work at all costs, don't speak up, call them or text them until they respond (even if that's a hundred times), etc. Pay attention to very panicked thoughts when you are activated.

If you tend to lean avoidant on the spectrum, notice thoughts you have about needing to do things alone or not being able to trust or rely on others. Also notice any negative thoughts about the relationship and your partner, especially thoughts that they are needy and clingy, or that they want too much from you.

The Practice

As always, the practice is the hard part. A lot of the practice of becoming more securely attached has to do with cultivating emotional safety in our relationships (as well as providing it to ourselves). Even if you don't currently have a romantic partner, you can practice this with friends and family.

Starting with some of the thought patterns you were able to pinpoint from the "Questions to Ask Yourself" section, are you able to challenge these thought patterns when you catch them? Can you take a breath and ask yourself, "What else could be true?" Are you able to level with yourself by asking, "Are these thoughts true? Or am I acting from a place of reactivity right now?"

If you find yourself feeling very activated, can you get up and into your body? Maybe take a mindful walk, do some mindful stretches, or jump up and down and shake it out. Getting into your body is a good way to get out of your head and calm your nervous system enough so that you can turn your logical mind back on.

The practice is the same when we start to connect the dots from our thoughts to our behaviors. If you aren't able to catch the thoughts before they turn into attachment-activated behaviors, can you pay more attention to certain ways you act or things you say and question them? Ask yourself, "Is this the way I want to be behaving in my ideal relationship?" If the answer is no, what kind of behavior would you prefer?

In the practice of challenging and changing unhealthy behaviors, it is incredibly helpful to first pinpoint the need underneath the behavior. What could your partner do or say in this moment that would calm you? Can you articulate for them the unmet need and the fear stemming from it (even if that feels wildly uncomfortable)?

For example, you find yourself texting or calling someone incessantly because they aren't responding. You know that the kind of relationship you truly desire is one where there is trust, security, and a sense of calm, so ask yourself what that would look like. First, put words to the activation happening inside of you as you keep texting or calling: "I am feeling so incredibly anxious right now because all I want is to hear from you that you are as committed to this relationship as I am, and because I can't get ahold of you, I have myself convinced that you don't feel that way." Then state what you need to hear: "I just need to hear from you that we're good."

Or let's say you are the one on the receiving end of the ten phone calls, voicemails, or texts, and you are ignoring them and fuming about how needy they are and how clearly they aren't the one for you. You know that the kind of relationship you truly desire is one where there is trust and an ability to communicate with each other in a way that feels mutual and respectful. Ask yourself what that would look like. Put words to your activation: "I am sensing your anxiety and desire for me to respond, and that is also giving me anxiety because I'm feeling overwhelmed." Then state what you need: "I am committed to this relationship, and I need an hour alone to just breathe. I promise to call you then and we can talk."

The anxious one is either going to be able to hear you and do their best to meet the need, or not. Either of these responses is information for you about their capacity to meet you at this point on your journey for inner growth.

*   *   *

This chapter has taken a super-simplified look at attachment styles. Since we're not going to be able to address all of the nuances here, we highly suggest that you do more research and work with your personal therapist on this stuff.

One last note, and it's a very important one: When your needs are being met in a relationship, your attachment style won't be as activated. And when your attachment style isn't activated, the relationship won't feel as dramatic and intense. Our nervous systems sometimes interpret this lack of drama as boredom and a lack of chemistry. Try to give it some time if you are questioning the attraction because of extended bouts of calm. It will take a lot of getting used to for your nervous system to register calm as healthy and to start to realize that in a secure attachment your needs are actually being met without a constant cycle of push-pull or highs and lows.

CHAPTER 11

How to Fight without Fighting

John

My parents are old-school Korean. They weren't raised to express and process their emotions. They were taught to push feelings down. My dad grew up dodging plates thrown by his dad, and my mom had screaming parents who should have never been together. Alcoholism ran rampant on both sides of the family. There was no such thing as self-help or AA meetings in Korea at that time. You just did what you could to survive.

When my own parents fought, Dad yelled. And Mom yelled back, until there was an explosion (usually from Dad). Then there was silence. And heavy tension. My brother stayed quiet and checked out. I was somewhere in the middle, part referee, part spectator, not knowing what to do. No one was ever heard. Nothing ever really got resolved. People just got loud and moved on.

I remember a story that my brother doesn't. Personally, I believe he may have suppressed it. One day, my dad came home to see my aunt crying. She was in tears because she had been cooking something stinky earlier when my brother brought his friends over. My brother got mad because he was embarrassed and he had yelled at her, making a cutting comment about how she should pay rent since she was living with us. I was underwater in our neighbor's pool when I saw my dad's shadow entering from the side of the house. As I came up for air, I heard his firm voice ordering my brother to return home. I got out of the pool and followed them. I hid in my bedroom and watched through the crack in the door. My aunt begged my dad to not hit my brother as my dad ordered him to remove his clothes. It was the first time I saw some North Korean shit in my house. My brother stripped down to his underwear, getting ready for his beating.

But my dad didn't do it. I wonder if he was feeling conflicted, between the old-school Korean ways of doing things (how he was raised) and what people did in America. It was the first glimmer I saw of him wanting to do things differently. But wanting to do things differently and actually doing them differently are two very, well, *different* things. My dad never saw a therapist or processed anything. He never acquired any tools. He never quit drinking until his later years, right before he passed. He continued to live as a walking reaction, emotionally hijacking spaces and verbally vomiting on people.

I wonder how much of that way of living rippled into

me, how much of it was learned and absorbed just from growing up under the same roof with my dad. Unlike addiction, which I do believe has a high genetic component, being reactive and prone to hijacking spaces comes more from nurture than nature. It's learned behavior that passes down, soaking into your body, conditioning you to think it's the norm. Then you grow up and realize it isn't. You go to school and see people interact with each other in softer, more grounded and caring ways. You go to friends' houses and see family arguments resolved without screaming or yelling. You wonder which way is the "right" way. I wonder how I would have been in my earlier relationships if my parents had been able to create safe spaces where we expressed our feelings and felt heard and understood. I wonder how many relationships could have been saved.

For most of my adult life, I have steamrolled my partners and not allowed them to be heard. Like I mentioned earlier, I would argue and pull from logic, focusing on being right rather than practicing empathy and truly trying to understand their heart and position—creating a safe space. I didn't know how to do otherwise. I never learned empathy and understanding. And even when I did, it was something I needed to practice. Over and over again, to undo the knee-jerk and unhealthy patterns ingrained in me.

Learning the how is like spotting decay in a tooth. You have to remove it—but that can take years of practice. And I think that's where most of us drop the ball. We don't practice. It's easier to practice with simple paint-by-number techniques.

Vanessa

When it comes to fighting, I have two modes: silence and stonewalling or verbal annihilation. As with everything, finding the middle ground is key for me (and for most of us). Neither of those extremes is healthy or conducive to a loving and stable relationship.

In my romantic relationships, I typically find myself on the silent end of the spectrum until I feel so completely unheard and cornered that I unleash. Thank God I had done enough work prior to meeting John that he has never been subjected to my verbal wrath. I'm embarrassed when I think of some of the things I have said or some of the ways I have spoken in the past to those I have claimed to love.

I find that a lot of other people are also guilty of this behavior. They use the idea of wanting to be "honest," to just "be themselves," to be able to say whatever is on their mind, as some sort of justification for being mean or using wildly unacceptable language in their fights. But even in your "telling it like it is," you are responsible for being kind. Attacking or being mean or belittling your partner is never a good thing, even if you're retaliating because they "did it first." How someone speaks to you in the worst moments of the relationship can be very telling of their character and their capacity to handle stress and emotional overwhelm.

NONVIOLENT COMMUNICATION

Besides the "fast elbows"—the three things to focus on to communicate better—nonviolent communication is another incredibly rich process that will help you understand how to fight without fighting, improve your overall ability to communicate, and increase the connectivity in your relationships, even when you and your partner seem to be at odds.

Nonviolent communication, or NVC, was developed by the psychologist Marshall B. Rosenberg. NVC works to bring us back into our natural state of giving and receiving in a compassionate manner, enabling us to lead from the heart. NVC connects us through empathy so we have more satisfying relationships. As Rosenberg puts it in the second edition of *Nonviolent Communication: A Language of Life*: "It guides us in reframing how we express ourselves and hear others" (p. 3). It is not a communication tool or a psychological theory, but rather a way of life. That's what makes it so powerful and sustainable.

We're going to summarize NVC here in a way that brings it down to street level, but we both highly recommend you read the book. There are also many trainings on the method available online.

First, the NVC process has four components:

Observations

Feelings

Needs

Requests

The observations component boils down to being able to reflect back what we are witnessing without evaluation or judgment—just the facts, if you will. The feelings component requires us to have an emotional vernacular in order to communicate how we feel about the observation we just reflected back. Needs, the third component, refers to our being able to then express the needs and desires that come from the feelings we have just identified. And the final component is making a clear and specific request around the need. These four components of nonviolent communication are practiced in both giving and receiving.

We want to clearly state that this process is not easy for most of us. We are not typically raised in a way that allows for healthy and open communication of hurt, desires, and needs, but with studying and practice we can integrate the four components of NVC into all areas of our everyday lives, not just in romantic relationships. Over time we begin to notice we're engaged in a more open-hearted and empathetic flow of communication that allows us to live and communicate from a more authentic place.

IT'S NEVER ABOUT THE WINE

I had been seeing Sam and Stella for about two months when a blowup happened in session. Up to that point they had been bringing to each therapy session the fights that had happened in the past week or the unprocessed and festering feelings around a fight from years earlier that had never been resolved. Essentially, Sam was not good at expressing needs and hurt feelings in a way that didn't come out as biting, cruel, and even condescending to Stella. In response, Stella almost never communicated anything. Instead, she swallowed it all and just got angrier and more passive-aggressive and nitpicky.

I was very clear with both of them early on that I could not predict if their relationship was salvageable or not, but that I could help them with things like communication. They had a son, Jude, and even if they ended their marriage, they were always going to be coparents to him. At a minimum, learning to be respectful of each other would help Jude (and them) in the long run. (Actually, what I think I said was "If we don't get to a place where we can at least be respectful of and to each other in our communication, I can promise you it will be Jude who suffers the most in the long run.")

During our fourth session, they were bickering about a confrontation from the night before. Stella had opened a bottle of wine from their wine fridge, and when Sam came in he got nasty about the specific bottle she had opened. He said some very hurtful things about her not listening to him and asked her if she was dumb. Apparently he had told her numerous times about a specific row of the fridge that held expensive wines reserved for special occasions, and that was one of the bottles she had opened on a random Tuesday for no other reason than to personally enjoy a glass.

Things were getting heated in the session, and it was becoming a ping-pong match of "Well, you always do this" and "You always do that" when I called a time-out. I began asking Sam deeper questions around his not feeling heard in the relationship. I was trying to understand more, but I was also modeling for Stella the process of asking deeper questions in order to open up a pathway to empathy and more vulnerable conversations. And to get out of the ping-pong match arguments that *never* went anywhere.

Sam began to cry. He expressed feeling deeply disrespected and misunderstood in his relationship. He didn't like speaking to Stella the way he did, and he didn't like the man he had become in this relationship, but he had no idea how to express his feelings of disconnection and sadness.

I prompted Stella to lean into this new turn of the conversation using the NVC techniques we had been practicing together in sessions. First, she observed and reflected back to Sam that she saw he was hurting and feeling disrespected. Then she shared that she felt deeply sorry that he was feeling that way. She expressed her desire to hear him talk about his feelings more frequently, not just in heated exchanges, because it would help her understand him better. She asked if, moving forward, he could attempt to use "I statements" about what he was feeling (for example, "I feel unheard/overlooked/dismissed/belittled"), rather than focus in on her, lashing out about her "behavior." Sam sat quietly throughout Stella's share, listening without trying to interrupt. The mood of the entire session shifted in that moment and stayed that way throughout the rest of our time together that day.

Did Stella's ability to tap into the steps of NVC in that moment save their entire relationship? No. But did it help them connect, hear the process under the content, and see each other in a much more vulnerable and human way in that moment? Yes. And that's the point. Challenging yourself to improve your communication skills won't magically make all of your relationships better overnight. It's a slow process, like building a house. You can't put ornate crown molding and a grand staircase into a house with a faulty foundation. I mean, you *can*. But wouldn't it be a terrible waste of beauty and time when that house crumbles in a windstorm?

APOLOGIZING FOR REALS

So many people believe they're apologizing when they're actually not. John and I witness it firsthand as therapists in our couples sessions. Step one of an apology needs to be, literally, just saying "I'm sorry." Nope. Doesn't happen. Those words rarely come out of people's mouths. And if they do, it's quickly followed by a "buttttt . . .," which negates anything that came before the "but," including the "I'm sorry."

John

> *The single biggest problem in communication is the illusion that it has taken place.*
>
> —GEORGE BERNARD SHAW

I totally understand why it's hard to apologize. I was one of those people. I never used to apologize. Instead, I would explain. The explanation would be my apology, so I got really good at explaining things. Usually to the point where the other person was so exhausted from listening to me explain that they didn't even want an apology anymore. They would rather I just stop talking.

My mother is like this too. She will explain for days instead of just saying two words. I've never heard her say "I'm sorry" in my life. Not once. So was my father. And also my brother. I do believe knowing how to apologize starts at home. Like manners. Apologizing if you hurt someone or did something wrong was never instilled in me. If you hurt someone or did something wrong, you explained to no end why you did what you did and you justified all of your actions in the process! So I grew up explaining a lot, rationalizing a lot, justifying a lot. This created distance, drift, and resentment in my relationships. I pulled from logic rather than heart.

It wasn't until recently—yes, around age forty-five, after a divorce, many expired relationships, getting a master's in psychology, and helping thousands of others apologize for reals—that I finally started to do it myself. And I'll be honest, it wasn't some fancy folded therapy technique I pulled out of my back pocket. I just asked myself: "If someone hurts me, would I want them to apologize? If so, how?" The answer was very simple. Yes. I would like them to just say, "I'm sorry." No explanation of why they said or did what they did. Just an honest, simple, heartfelt "I'm sorry." After saying that, they could explain—but only if their "I'm sorry" was followed by an "and," not a "but."

Then I asked myself: "How important would this be to me? How would this make me feel about the other person?" I realized that hearing a real apology would be extremely important to me, because it would allow me to trust the other person and know that they could take ownership of their actions. Because, if you don't own your stuff, you don't grow. Then I wondered, if they didn't apologize, how would that affect how I felt about them and the relationship? Well, it would push me away; I wouldn't trust them as much.

As I answered these questions, I thought about all my ex-girlfriends whom I never apologized to. I thought about what it must have made them feel like and how that impacted our relationship. I suddenly had a revelation that something as simple as an apology might have changed a lot of things.

Vanessa is the first partner I can honestly say I have apologized to for reals. Sure, I still explain myself. But I make sure I apologize for hurting her first. I end that apology with a period. Then, if it serves the relationship to understand where I was coming from, I offer the explanation. I notice how apologizing first and explaining later lowers our guards, letting us communicate from a place of love again. Instead of from our wounds. It prevents reactions and creates responses. I also notice how it encourages Vanessa to hit the ball back. Once she feels heard, she takes ownership and apologizes for her piece. The simple act of saying you're sorry can prevent fights from turning into blowups. "Sorry" creates bridges instead of walls.

Vanessa

When I was growing up, apologies usually sounded something like "I'm sorry we fought" instead of "I'm sorry I said X, Y, and Z. That was wrong of me, and I know it hurt your feelings." The words "I'm sorry" were said, but the ownership wasn't really there in many ways. A true apology comes from ownership. If we don't own something, then we don't have to do the hard work of growing and changing. Then, when we do or say it again later, we won't feel bad about it, or we can even hang it over the other person's head when it seems like a convenient strategy to win a fight.

It's not surprising then that I struggle to own my very specific part in something that caused hurt to someone else, or really just to articulate that at all. I've apologized for my part here and there along my journey, but never in a consistent way. I'd never been held accountable for a real apology until I met John. I'd never known that my apology wouldn't be used as ammo against me at a later date, until I met John. I'd never felt safe enough that I could own my part in something without feeling like it meant I was a bad person, until I met John.

Apologizing for reals shouldn't be based on the other person's response, but feeling safe does help you apologize. I realize now that it was in the way John apologized to me that he showed me I could do it too. He would say, "I'm sorry," get specific, and then not defend himself in a way that made me feel like I could do the same. If he felt safe enough to do that with me, then I could do it with him too.

Like every topic we have covered and will keep covering, so many of these things are a two-way street. An extra tip if you want to be a better apologizer: spend more time with people who are good apologizers. Pay attention to how a real apology makes you feel. And then cultivate the desire to give that feeling to another person. This practice takes the apology out of the place of your ego, or your pride, and into the place of wanting to make the person on the other side feel safe, seen, held, and loved.

Now, having said all that, I admit that I'm by no means perfect at apologizing. I still struggle. I still feel shame, and my pride still digs in its heels sometimes. As someone who has struggled to communicate her feelings and needs for most of her life, it can sometimes feel like I'm *always* the one apologizing. The pattern can look like this: Vanessa says/does something . . . which leads to John sitting her down and bringing it up . . . which leads to Vanessa feeling shame but still owning it and apologizing . . . which leads to Vanessa walking away feeling like her side hasn't been heard and is never heard, that she is the screwup in the relationship, and that she isn't really being understood.

It is so so so important to notice when I start feeling this pattern developing. The pattern of feeling like "the doormat," or "the screwup," or the one responsible for all of the change in order to keep the relationship going without further conflict. Because, when the pattern shows up, it typically means I am not speaking up. That I am falling into old ways of living with resentments and playing peacekeeper. That I need to recommit to my practice of noticing hurt feelings or behavior patterns that I don't feel good about and bringing them to John, rather than convincing myself they aren't worth mentioning and waiting for him to be the one to bring things to me (and then being surprised and annoyed when he does and feeling like the screwup—insert cycle).

If this is a pattern of yours, it is important that your side be heard, even if you're the one apologizing. But apologizing in the moment, followed by a "but . . .," is not typically the way to go. Because anything after "but" negates what came before it. An apology can only be made after a moment of true acceptance of your part, of where you can own your shortcoming in that moment and a true consideration of what you plan to do about it moving forward.

SORRY ISN'T ENOUGH

As we mentioned earlier, saying "I'm sorry" is only step one. It's only one side of the coin. The other side is to take action. Just saying you're sorry isn't enough. Simply put: What are you going to do about it now? "I'm going to dig in and work on my jealous feelings instead of blaming you." "I'm going to take a minute and try to think before I react like that." "I'm going to make an effort to remember our anniversary." "I'm going to process my shit with a therapist so I don't put it on you anymore." "I'm going to take an anger management course." Only with action comes change.

When two people apologize for reals—saying they're sorry and then taking some kind of action—they begin to lay new tracks in the relationship. Old patterns can be broken. It's one of the quickest ways to shift a relationship, and it sounds so simple. But our ego and our desire to always be right makes it hard to do. We're not used to letting go of the tug-of-war rope. For most of us, defensiveness and self-protection is the only gear we know.

Questions to Ask Yourself

If you're new to this and saying the words "I'm sorry" makes you cringe, sit with the cringe. What feelings does apologizing bring up? What thoughts start to race when you are faced with owning your part in something? It's really important to pay attention to this in order to get to the root of your aversion to apologizing. Is it shame, as Vanessa struggles with? Is it pride? Is it a feeling of worthlessness? Anger?

There is a lot of shame tied up in apologizing for many of us. Saying "I'm sorry" brings up feelings of being "bad" or not enough. Whatever the feeling is, acknowledge it and seek to understand the source. And then say the words "I'm sorry" anyway, even if feelings of shame or defensiveness or embarrassment come along with them. You can't get better at something without trying it again and again.

The Practice

Obviously, the first part of the practice is actually saying the words "I'm sorry for (what I did or said). I will try to (not do or say that) moving forward." If you struggle at first with owning what you did or said, try at least to acknowledge and apologize for how you made the other person feel. If you find yourself either cringing at the thought of apologizing or being the one constantly demanding one, it also might be helpful to ask yourself if you are trying to have these conversations when things are too heated. When we first start practicing healthy communication skills, especially if they are completely new and foreign to us, we will probably find ourselves getting heated and overwhelmed very quickly. It is completely okay to ask for time to walk away and cool down. I like to tell clients that they should come up with a safe word or phrase that means a time-out is needed when either person is feeling flooded.

Flooded: Becoming so overwhelmed by your feelings that your prefrontal cortex goes offline and you begin to act only from a state of survival. When you are flooded, higher modes of thinking and feeling, such as empathy, are almost impossible to access.

There are two important things about the practice of taking a time-out to cool down: a time-out can be called at any time, and the person asking for the time-out is not responsible for explaining why they need one. The other person has to respect the need for a time-out. But here's what the person asking for the time-out is responsible for: they have to communicate how long they need before they can try to continue the conversation. Ten minutes? An hour? Twenty-four hours? Any amount of time is fine, but a time frame has to be given. And both of them have to commit to resuming the conversation after that time elapses.

The second part is seeing if you can use the tools we practiced in chapter 9 and in the section on nonviolent communication in this chapter. Can you put words to the subtext, the process? Can you reflect back to the other person the hurt that you hear them expressing to you? Bonus points if you can offer the apology and the reflection without being asked for it. Pull from some of the parts of NVC, making them your own. All of these tools are helpful and can be played with until you find the mixture that feels the most authentic and helpful to you. Be aware that you probably won't do this "right" the first time or even the first twenty times. That's okay. It's important to do this practice even if you feel like you are stumbling, getting it wrong, or looking stupid. Maybe even admit that feeling to the other person. There is a potential for even more vulnerability and connection in speaking truth to your struggle.

Third, don't use the word "but" in the same conversation as your "I'm sorry." Try your best to bite your tongue and allow the conversation to be only about the other person's experience in that moment. Hear them out. Own what's yours. Continue to monitor and notice the emotions and thoughts that come up for you around this experience, but try not to make it about you. Take a breath, take a beat, take a walk. See if you can take some time to be with yourself. Take whatever space you need to be able to articulate what you would have said if you were allowed to say "but" in the moment. If you were allowed to explain yourself at the expense of the apology. Instead, replace the "but" (even in your head) with "and." The other person's feelings are valid *and* you also have a feeling or a hurt or a need that is worthy of being expressed. Then ask the other person if you can discuss your "and." The reason for taking a beat to sit with your "and" is to make sure it's not simply being pulled from a place of defense and is actually something that feels important to communicate and for the other person to know about you and where you were coming from.

PART 3

Build Something Sustainable

Water seeks its own level, and water rises collectively.

—Julia Cameron

Okay, so you have collided with each other and examined the chemistry to see if it's coming from a healthy place. You have explored your love patterns and emotional wounds. You are swimming past the breakers and learning how to fight without fighting. Now it's time to build something sustainable and lasting.

John

It hit me while Vanessa was away leading a retreat in Arizona. Since I would be on daddy duty for a full week by myself, which I'd never done before, we had planned for her mother to fly out and help me. We also had two babysitters as backup. Everything was taken care of. She was good to go. No big deal.

But one day before Vanessa left, her mother found out she had been exposed to someone with Covid, and she didn't want to put our daughter at risk. So there went Mom. Then the babysitters we had on call called out. Both of them. At least I had Logan's school. That would give me half a day to work and work out and have some time for myself to reboot. Well, the first day Vanessa was gone, school shut down for a week because a teacher had Covid. So there I was, alone with a toddler who had never been away from her mother for more than one night. I made a decision. I wasn't going to complain. I wasn't going to pout. I wasn't going to make Vanessa feel guilty or strip her of this experience, something she had been putting together for nearly a year.

I had shit on my eyebrows from a squirming two-year-old not wanting Daddy to wipe her butt because only "Mommy do it!!" The heat in the house went out when I accidentally tapped an auto-shut-off earthquake lever while putting the garbage cans away. And finally, I accidentally put in the wrong address for the food delivery, so I overpaid for someone else's dinner. That's about the time some feelings started coming up. Anger. Resentment. This wasn't the deal. I wasn't supposed to be doing this alone. Also, Vanessa wasn't checking on me every two minutes like the old John that was being activated wished she was. And that meant she didn't care. She didn't appreciate me. I felt lost, overwhelmed, and alone.

This is where the road forked and I had a choice to make. I could be reactive. Passive-aggressive. Make her feel guilty for leaving. I could set off her panic button without it appearing intentional and maybe even get her to come home early. Or. I could figure it out. Do my best. No one was going to die from a little shit on their face. Literally. This could be an opportunity to spend some quality time with my daughter because when Mommy is here she's usually clinging to her leg.

I'm not going to lie. It was a hard week, and it went by root canal slow, but I got through it. The revelation came on the very last day, when Logan and I were hanging a WELCOME HOME, MOMMY sign that we (me) had painted. I realized that being able to not complain, to make sure to ask Vanessa about her experience and how she was doing, and to take care of my own shit and feelings without putting them on her didn't just come from the tools I've acquired throughout the years in therapy rooms. It came from the safe container of the relationship Vanessa and I had both built. I'm sure she was going through her own inner struggles during her week away that she owned and didn't put on me. This was the first knowing I had that our relationship was sustainable. That we had built something with sturdy legs.

You may be thinking, so you went a week with no child care while your partner was away working and you guys didn't get into a fight. What's the big deal? That makes your relationship sustainable? First, let me say, it was ten days, not seven. And second, yes. How we come to the knowing that our relationship has legs is different for everyone. For someone else, it may come after a fight with no chairs thrown or no character assassination. Or after sex that wasn't just about skin hunger but about both parties feeling present and seen and connected. For me, it was getting through ten days alone with my daughter and not complaining or harboring resentment. Also appreciating everything Vanessa does as a mother by walking in her shoes. It made me feel closer to her. It made me trust us. More.

Vanessa

For months leading up to my retreat I was anxious about leaving John and Logan. Would they be okay? Would he remember to feed her vegetables and brush her teeth? Would she have a hard time without me there? Would he be mad at me for going? Could I focus on what I was doing without being consumed by worry about what was going on at home? I had worked so hard on executing the retreat that I knew, no matter what, I was going. Even after my mom had to cancel at the last minute. Even after finding out that school would be closed. No matter how hard it would be, I knew there would be many lessons in this, for all three of us.

The first few days were rough. I slept like shit and had a hard time being present. John texted me a few times about the meltdowns Logan was having, or the issues he was having with her. He sent me videos of them at the park at three in the afternoon, and she was still in her pajamas. My best friend and copilot at the retreat was there to hold me down and make sure I didn't bring my knee-jerk response to these messages. "They're fine, Vanessa. So what if her pajamas are on, she's alive. Also, I wish he wasn't sending you messages about her melting down. Just handle it, John, let Vanessa be here fully. This is good for him, Vanessa. He also needs to trust in himself too that he can handle this alone." This was part of her daily morning pep talk to me.

All kinds of deeply rooted overfunctioning and co-dependent shit came up for me that week. Did I trust John to parent our daughter? Did I trust him to hold down the fort and manage the home? Could I allow myself the experience of being present for myself and my career and something I had been building? Could I focus on just one thing without needing the adrenaline of being pulled in multiple directions at once? And one of the biggest things I had to face—could I finally shed the belief that I was always just the girlfriend on the sidelines who supported whatever her man was doing or building?

I have always been very career- and goal-driven. I climbed up the ladder in advertising and was making six figures while managing a large team and three multimillion-dollar accounts by the time I was twenty-nine. I worked my ass off. At my job. But all of the men I had seriously dated (including John) had a passion, an art, something they did outside of their work that gave back to the world and that also tended to put them on center stage. And while they were fulfilling that side of themselves, I was watching them shine from the wings and bitching about being unhappy about my job. I always loved supporting them, don't get me wrong, but there was always a small part of me that knew I had something inside of me to share that wasn't just social media campaigns and TV commercials for beverage brands and beauty lines.

So the week I was away I faced not only my unfounded belief that I was the only one who could do it all, and do it *right*, for my daughter, but also my hope that I could step into my power, lead something that was truly mine and only mine, and be supported by my partner from the sidelines. Without getting his ego bruised, or feeling emasculated by it. Without him making me feel guilty for prioritizing myself.

It was in that recognition that I had a deep knowing that this partnership was different from all of the others. My learning was this: John supported me in a way I had never experienced before by stepping up that week and making sure I knew that my dreams and my passions were just as much a priority as his. Not just that I knew that myself, but that I knew that *he* felt that way too.

That is the kind of relationship I've always wanted— the kind that to me equals sustainability. It's not just in coparenting well and having good sex and being able to fight without fighting. For me, a partnership is sustainable if you support each other in the things that make you truly feel alive. If each of you can step back, prop the other up, and let the other fully shine. And then truly shine just watching the other shine. That's what gives a relationship wings.

CHAPTER 12

I'm Not Your Mother, You're Not My Son

I f we had a nickel for every time a client, a friend, or we ourselves complained about one person in a partnership "not doing enough," "nagging them," "making them feel inadequate," "acting like a child," "treating them like a child," and on and on, we would be multimillionaires living on a private island somewhere.

Because we are two cisgender people in a heterosexual relationship, we are going to speak to the under- and overfunctioner dance from that perspective. In many instances, but not always, it can show up gendered (the woman being the overfunctioner and the man being the underfunctioner) in heterosexual relationships. Many of these roles have been socialized into us by the society we have been raised in. This does not mean that those who don't fall into this narrow heterosexual category do not struggle with this pattern. As therapists, we've seen it present itself in same-sex couples and in the opposite genders as well.

First, let's break down what overfunctioning and underfunctioning actually are. Both are behavioral responses to anxiety, to the fear of vulnerability and getting hurt, and both reflect a struggle with communicating needs. They are both learned, through family and society, and practiced until they become deeply ingrained ways of relating in relationships. If I am uncomfortable with other people's struggle, with things not being under control or done a specific way, with my fear of the unknown, with the feeling that comes with the deep desire to be taken care of and truly seen, I will most likely overfunction as a way to soothe these anxieties.

On the flip side, if I am uncomfortable with being connected to my emotions, have feelings around inadequacy, don't believe I have the ability or resilience to take care of myself or others, and feel like I'm not good enough, I will most likely underfunction as a response to these anxieties and beliefs.

So what do these behaviors look like in action? Here are some examples:

OVERFUNCTIONING

- Finishing people's sentences when they're struggling

- Giving advice to a stressed-out friend who hasn't asked for any

- Always picking the restaurant for your friend group

- Reminding people they should hurry up and book travel

- Doing something for your child that they can do, so it will create less of a mess

- Doing something for someone they can do, because you're faster or better at it

- Keeping a mental schedule for your partner because they often forget appointments

- Not sharing important beliefs or opinions to prevent making others anxious

- Creating a secret alternative plan when you know someone will mess up

- Explaining someone else's thinking in a work meeting when they're present

- Buying someone a self-help book you've recommended

- Doing something for someone even after they've communicated they're capable

- Being a backseat driver

- Constantly checking in with someone who's agreed to take on a project

- Leaving instructions for a job that a person could easily figure out themselves

- Furiously completing tasks for others when you feel anxious or distressed

- Talking a lot to fill in the gaps and awkward pauses in conversations

- Steering your child away from experiences that may result in failure

- Worrying about other people's responsibilities

UNDERFUNCTIONING

- Avoiding daily tasks that you're not good at because you don't want to be seen as incompetent

- Refusing to learn how to do new things because your partner has always done them for you in the past

- Asking for permission from your partner to eat junk food

- Allowing your partner to handle the taxes every year because you don't understand the process and don't really want to

- Asking a co-worker for help on a project that you know you can do yourself, but don't trust you will do it to the standard your boss likes

- Spending hours on social media rather than solving the tasks at hand because you're feeling overwhelmed by how much is on your plate

- Knowing that you won't clean the bathroom the way your partner likes it to be done, so you don't bother

- Knowing you have been called irresponsible, careless, or immature by family or a partner

- Having an unorganized desk or workspace

- Not making the bed because you assume your partner will or because you don't believe you can do it right

Just like many of the other dynamics where it seems that opposites attract, under- and overfunctioners *love* each other. We are unconsciously drawn to each other because we activate the shit out of each other! No, but seriously, our unconscious seeks out the activation for three reasons.

First, it's what feels normal. If I am an overfunctioner with an underfunctioner, then I'm with someone who allows me to overfunction. I can play my role, stay in my lane, in my comfort zone, doing the thing I know I'm good at. In this way I can add value to the relationship, be needed, be worthy.

Second, both under- and overfunctioners want to embody some of the qualities the other has that they struggle with themselves. We wish we had some of what they have so naturally.

And finally, we're in the grip of repetition compulsion— the pull to repeat past traumas and patterns over and over again in the hope that we will somehow solve the puzzle, get it right, or heal the wound this time. Frankly, these are the same three reasons underlying the attraction of opposites in any of the dynamics we've talked about in this book.

Going into a relationship unaware of your attachment style, your love languages, how you're wired to fight, and your over- or underfunctioning tendencies can, at best, be a major rub in your relationship and, at worst, be the reason you end up hating what you first loved about your partner.

Vanessa

> *Like a seesaw, it is the under-functioning of one individual that allows for the over-functioning of the other. . . . Under-functioners and over-functioners provoke and reinforce each other's behaviour, so that the seesaw becomes increasingly hard to balance over time.*
>
> —HARRIET LERNER, *THE DANCE OF ANGER*

Ex: Shut the fuck up.

Me: I'm sorry, what the fuck did you just say to me?

Ex: Shut. The. Fuck. Up.

Me: I'm taking the dog for a walk. While I'm gone, you need to find another place to live.

Sadly, this was one of the last exchanges between me and my ex-fiancé before the official ending of a relationship that neither of us knew how to keep alive anymore. Years of over- and underfunctioning had finally come to a head (among many, many other unhealthy patterns and dynamics). I nitpicked, he got defensive. I was passive-aggressive, he got verbally aggressive. As I became more outright controlling and codependent, he fluctuated between withdrawal and anger. Because I had no idea how to get my needs met, I felt perpetually unsafe, and so I controlled, controlled, controlled.

Until recently, I never had a grasp on what I call my "mothering." The why, the how, the ability to recognize it before, during, and after, how to own it and apologize for it, how to get my needs met or self-soothe without having to go there at all (still working on this one). I have personally done every single one of those things on the overfunctioning list in the last section. Every single one. Without my own therapy and a partner who is committed to showing up and challenging me on it without turning to character assassination and aggression, I would have continued to be controlled by my unconscious drive to control things and people in order to manage my own anxiety.

I am always moving, always scanning for danger, always planning and overplanning to manage as much of the outcome as I can, as well as the anxiety of everyone around me. It. Is. Exhausting. I struggle with burnout, overwhelm, and resentment. And not just in my romantic relationships. This shit shows up in my family and friend relationships and at work as well. In hindsight I can see how it has affected all of my relationships for years.

I can also see so clearly my ten-year-old self, feeling like it was my role to try to take care of my baby brother, to try to emotionally care-take and give some peace to my exhausted mother, and to start trying, already, to control the outcomes of all interactions with my friends. Whether or not all this was actually my responsibility is not the point. The point is that at a very young age I felt that it was my responsibility. I felt that if I took on all of this responsibility myself, my loved ones would be safer and happier. And I got a lot of praise for my behavior. I remember being told so many times how helpful I was, how grown-up I was, how good a kid I was. It was cemented into me at a very young age that being helpful, being needed, and being good was how I received praise and love, and until about the age of thirty-five I never questioned the strategies that came from that belief.

Here's another very unfun side effect when the over- and underfunctioning dynamic shows up in your romantic relationships: there is no greater libido killer than feeling like your partner is your child or your parent.

The Belgian psychotherapist Esther Perel says that we are biologically wired not to mate with our parents or children. So when the relationship dynamic turns into a parental one, naturally the sexual desire wanes. If there was ever a reason to dig in and understand and then challenge your over- and underfunctioning behaviors, this might be it.

John

A running joke I tell often is how I used to ask my ex-wife if I could buy sugar cereal. She wanted healthy "adult" cereal, and I wanted Lucky Charms. But instead of expressing myself and making my own decisions, I would ask her for permission and beg her. It's not funny actu-

ally. It's sad. What I didn't realize I was doing was cementing the mother-child dynamic, or in this case, the
overfunctioner-underfunctioner dynamic. Of course, over
time this changed the chemistry of the relationship. I went
from her mouth to her nipple.

When we first started dating, she saw a kid in his twenties managing a dozen employees of a trendy restaurant
bar, making indie films, writing screenplays, and taking
on passion projects. She saw that I was ambitious and a
leader. Then when we moved in together she saw another
side of me. Not making my bed, peeing in the shower,
and eating like a child. It's not that I changed after we
got together. She just didn't see all of who I was until we
moved in and started doing life together. This is evidence
that underfunctioning doesn't have anything to do with
the scoreboard or how successful a person is. It has to do
with their emotional functioning and how being stunted
and insecure ripples into their behavior. And ultimately
that ripples into the dynamic of their relationships.

Thinking about it, I can see that a theme in all my relationships has been that my partners took care of me on
some level more than what was healthy. I'm not sure how
I became an underfunctioner. There seem to be many
layers to it. First, I grew up as the youngest sibling. By
contrast, my older brother had to grow up fast. He was
helping my parents pay bills and run the family business
at age fifteen. He was my umbrella. I was shielded from
responsibility and got to go out and play with friends all
day. I never acquired the tools to be responsible. I never

had chores, curfews, or consequences—all of which teach discipline and values and build a sense of worth.

I also didn't get a lot of emotional milk, which I think is another layer. My parents never told me I could do things. They never showed a belief in me that instilled a belief in myself. So I grew up with a core belief that I wasn't good at anything. That I needed to be taken care of. That I was the "almost guy." Under the underfunctioning is the deep belief that you "can't."

Questions to Ask Yourself

Even though the topic of over- and underfunctioning could fill an entire book, it isn't something we learned about in therapy school. We're pretty sure that, until Brené Brown talked about under- and overfunctioning in her book *The Gifts of Imperfection: Let Go of Who You Think You're Supposed to Be and Embrace Who You Are*, neither of us had ever even heard the terms before. If you want to do further digging, start with psychologist Murray Bowen's family systems theory. It was Bowen who coined the terms. You can also explore this dynamic in Harriet Lerner's book *The Dance of Connection*.

Regardless of which side of the coin you fall on, the key to understanding and then unraveling over- and under-functioning patterns is to get really curious about the payoff. What is the benefit from the behaviors you're performing? Both of them serve a purpose. They give you something, or you wouldn't be doing them. Answering this question takes work because it can be hard for us to be real with ourselves. It's hard to follow the thread down to the fears that drive over- and underfunctioning behaviors, and it's much easier to make it about the other person and what they are or are not doing.

IF YOU'RE AN OVERFUNCTIONER

Brown says that, "for overfunctioners, it is easier to do than to feel," so the questions and practices for you are going to be all about going inward, getting in touch with the feeling, the emotions, the things you are trying to bypass by doing, doing, doing. Unfortunately, the work in ending this unhealthy dance usually starts with you. The underfunctioner does not have to function if you are doing it all for them. Why would they? It's a pretty sweet deal if you think about it.

If you find yourself feeling overwhelmed and resentful, pay close attention to when those feelings bubble up and ask yourself, simply put: What are you doing that you should not be doing? If you know you shouldn't be doing it, why are you doing it then? Does it stress you out that what you're doing won't be done the "right" way or the way you like it to be done? Are you worried that something catastrophic will happen if you aren't involved? Do you not trust the other person to do it, or do you expect them to disappoint you? Are you avoiding asking for help? *Be honest.*

For example, when I (Vanessa) get into my overfunctioning pattern in parenting our daughter and I am annoyed that John isn't "pulling his weight" with parenting, I have to be honest with myself and ask: "Where am I doing too much and not asking him for more? Why? If I truly back

off and let him handle it, what am I worried will happen?"
Letting John do it won't look the way it would if I did it,
but will our daughter *die*? Ninety-nine percent of the time
(I won't say 100 percent!), the answer to that question is an
obvious "no." So then I have to check myself and back the
hell off and allow him to step in and do it his way.

It's good that I'm anxious and stressed out about it, because those are emotions I can sit with and examine and feel.
Just like Brené Brown says. It's those emotions I'm trying to
avoid by overfunctioning in the first place. And guess what?
If I never force myself to sit in them, I won't ever learn how
to manage and survive them. That's how emotions work,
unfortunately.

IF YOU'RE AN UNDERFUNCTIONER

> *Underfunctioners should look at the ways that under-*
> *functioning keeps them in the myth of their lack of*
> *power . . . their smallness . . . their dependence. It's*
> *disempowering. They need to look at their own resentment*
> *about the condescending nature of someone functioning*
> *for them and ask themselves do they want to be parented*
> *forever? Is that a turn on? That type of thing.*
>
> —DENÉ LOGAN, AMFT

Underfunctioners appear to get less competent under
stress, and so they step back and allow others to take over.
Just like there are benefits for overfunctioners in doing
it all, there are benefits for you as the underfunctioner.
Sometimes the benefits for the underfunctioner seem

more obvious. To the outside world you seem to be the one who "does less" in the relationship and has someone who will manage it all—physically, emotionally, and mentally. But in reality, in your inner world, you are keeping yourself stunted by stepping back and allowing others to overfunction for you.

The questions for you are going to be around building and strengthening your self-esteem and getting more in touch with your strengths and competencies. So get honest with yourself. How have you benefited in your life and relationships from allowing others to carry the load (especially the emotional load)? On the flip side, do you feel like allowing that has kept you small and dependent on others? How and what has this behavior kept you believing about yourself? What are you worried will happen if you step up and out, speak up and take ownership of the areas of your life in which you underfunction?

The Practice

The bottom line is that if you stay in an over- and under-functioning dance, neither of you can ever grow or reach your full potential in the relationship. There will always be a power differential where one person feels parental and the other feels childlike. And this dynamic simply cannot exist in healthy romantic relationships (at least not consistently). In a healthy partnership, both of you need to feel like you can lean into the other, that your weaknesses are complemented by your partner's strengths, that you are a team standing shoulder to shoulder.

Once you have asked yourself the questions, the practice is about repeating these three steps:

- Continuing to tap into and heighten your awareness of over- or underfunctioning behavior. Noticing when it happens, pausing and breathing into that awareness, and being kind to yourself in your repeating of the habit as you learn to break it.

- Asking yourself the questions here over and over again. Why do you over- or underfunction? What does this behavior serve? What are you scared will happen?

- Being open with your partner about what you notice about yourself through the first two steps here. Have conversations about your behavior and the reasons for it that you are discovering and trying to challenge. Ask for your partner's help in this effort. Speak up about what you need and why. Communicate. Be vulnerable.

CHAPTER 13

Fuck *The Giving Tree*: On Codependency

Caution: If you trade in your authenticity for being liked, you may experience the following: anxiety, depression, addiction, rage, blame, resentment and inexplicable grief.

—BRENÉ BROWN

Like most people, we loved *The Giving Tree* by Shel Silverstein when we were growing up. But the older we got, and the more aware of relationship dysfunction, the more we realized how much that book reads more like a *How to Become Codependent, for Beginners*. The basic story (spoiler alert) is boy and tree love each other, and boy loves playing under and in the tree. Boy grows up and stops playing with the tree but still comes back occasionally to visit and express his more grown-up desires: money, a house, family, and travel. The tree gives him her apples to sell, her branches to build his house, and finally her entire trunk to build a boat. In the end the tree has nothing left to give and is just a stump, where the then old man rests.

On the surface *The Giving Tree* seems like a beautiful story of love and sacrifice, but what is it really teaching us about relationships? That it is normal and even celebrated to give and give and give of yourself without any reciprocity, until you are nothing but a sad and lonely stump.

Understanding codependency and how it creeps into almost every area of our relational lives is exceptionally important on this journey we call life. At least if you are anything like us and are trying to live the most fulfilling and authentic life possible. The field of codependency research is broad and has evolved a lot over the past fifty or so years since it was first discussed as a way to classify the personalities and behaviors exhibited by the wives of the alcoholic husbands in AA.

We now understand codependency as so much more than an issue for wives of alcoholic men. The problem is, there are so many different definitions of codependency out there, and it is used out of context and incorrectly in our social media wellness world so often, that it can be hard to pinpoint. Here is the definition that we use when discussing codependency: "If you're good, I'm good. If you're not good, I'm not good." It's that simple. Your emotional state is based on someone else's emotional state. You also find your sense of self and sense of worth in someone else. The list of codependent "symptoms" is long, but they all stem from the same place: a deep-rooted fear of abandonment or rejection, and shame.

So what are some basic ways to understand how code-pendency can show up and wreak havoc in your romantic relationships? Vanessa could talk about this for days, but she's going to try her best to summarize some of the most helpful thoughts, learnings, and tips for anyone who wants to move from a codependent way of relating to others to a place of more interdependence. Meaning that both of you prioritize self-care and boundaries, you feel safe to express yourself and ask for your needs to be met, and you're open to hearing your partner's thoughts, feelings, and needs. You also understand that your partner cannot meet all of your needs, just as you can't meet all of theirs, and knowing this doesn't make you feel less worthy as a partner.

Vanessa

My codependency recovery journey was jump-started when I finally woke up and realized that my ex had an alcohol problem. I remember the exact moment, probably five years into our relationship. My mom was visiting for the weekend. She picked up a one-liter bottle of Kettle One vodka from our liquor shelf and stared at it. "Didn't you just get this bottle as a gift two weeks ago at your party?"

"Yes," I replied.

She turned it over on its side, wide-eyed. "Vanessa, there is less than a quarter of the bottle left."

"I know, but I also have some in a flask hidden in the back of the freezer so that I can have some too."

She just looked at me. "Oh."

In my head, a light bulb went off. Oh, so it's not normal to have to hide alcohol in a separate container from your significant other so that you can have a little too since they will consume the entire bottle in two weeks without even asking if you want any?

To be fair, my codependent personality was in place long before I met that ex, and it remains in place to this day. But it took starting therapy and then grad school while being in that relationship for all of the pieces to fall into place and give me a few major wake-up moments that pushed me into my recovery journey.

Codependent behaviors develop in childhood as a way to defend against the potential for rejection and abandonment. Listen, 99 percent of our parents aren't assholes. They are human beings who did the best they could with what they had, *and* there were still behaviors in our families growing up that affected our ability to show up authentically or caused us to feel like we had to emotionally take care of our parent(s). You didn't have to suffer physical abuse or grow up with an addicted parent to develop codependent tendencies (though of course that helps), but having your emotions dismissed or belittled, being told that you and your emotions were too much, having a parent whose go-to was the cold shoulder, having a parent who hovered and did everything for you, never allowing you to fail or screw up—these are all examples of how seemingly small behaviors add up over a lifetime to what might be called developmental traumas. It took me years and working with dozens of clients on specific codependent tendencies to also realize that basically all of us struggle with some form of these behaviors in one relationship or another, or at some point in our life. We are raised, as a society, to be codependent.

When I met John, I thought I had cracked the code! He didn't struggle with any substances, so that was it—I'm cured! Yeah, that's not how it works at all. John has just as much of a compulsive personality as any of the other men I've dated. He just doesn't use substances. Instead, he uses things like working out and sugar to soothe anxiety, numb hard feelings, or escape reality. The personality structure is still similar in him, and it's clearly part of what I was unconsciously drawn to. There is something in a compulsive personality that says it needs to be saved, fixed, or taken care of. And boy do codependents love to be needed.

We don't have to check the box on every single trait of codependency to know that we struggle with it. For me, in my relationship with John, it shows up in several ways: in my role as the "don't rock the boat" girl; in my deep struggle to communicate my needs or really even know what they are, to articulate them at all; in the deep feeling of shame I feel when John tries to discuss with me any area I could improve in our relationship; in my go-to behavior around caretaking and overfunctioning and trying to do everything alone until I am consumed with feelings of resentment for having to do it all alone (being the doormat); and in so so many other ways.

I don't react in the same ways I did when I was in my last relationship. I am so much more aware of it all now, but that doesn't mean I don't still struggle. In my opinion, codependent behaviors don't disappear. We slowly get better and better at being in the discomfort of showing up fully and asking for what we need regardless of our fear of how the other person might respond. And we get better and better at it through doing it. Through exposure. We can read all the books in the world, but the bottom line is that, like any inner healing, it only starts to cement when we change the behaviors, when we choose to do things differently regardless of the emotional risk.

Even as I write this, I am fully aware that I have needs I have a hard time expressing to John. For many of us who struggle with codependency, coming to a true understanding of the Self can be a long journey, one that we might not even know how and where to begin. Knowing our needs and our desires is an important building block in the relationship we have with our Self. For many of us, we have to back our way into knowing our needs, meaning that we develop our needs in response to what we are not getting.

I'll give you a personal example: I did not know that emotional consistency and reassurance were needs of mine until I was able to pinpoint them when John sometimes gets moody or dark, when he pulls inside and emotionally freezes me out. Even if his behavior has nothing to do with me, it makes me feel like I have done something wrong and sends me into a full-blown anxiety spiral. While I am simultaneously doing my own work to not personalize things like other people's emotions (another symptom of codependency), I have also expressed to him that when he is in a weird headspace and needs to disconnect for a while, he only needs to tell me that's what is happening with him and remind me that it's not about us or me. Once he does that, I am able to give him the space and even provide empathy and compassion, without feeling totally unstable myself.

It's not even that I am actively choosing not to express my needs. It's that they don't even register with me as needs until either I'm really upset about something and realize it has something to do with unmet needs, or John starts a tough conversation and opens up the lines of communication. Then, all of a sudden, I realize that there are needs I haven't been paying attention to that I should also speak up about.

I've spent a lifetime so focused on everyone else that I don't actually know what my own needs and wants are until they metaphorically hit me over the head. I'm getting better, but it's a journey to know yourself deeply.

Questions to Ask Yourself

If you struggle with codependent behaviors now and then, trust me, you're not alone in this. We all struggle sometimes, even if we don't identify as a codependent. Codependent behavior isn't black and white but rather more of a spectrum. (See the box on codependence, hyper-independence, and interdependence.) And most of the time it's not just one person in the relationship who struggles while the other person doesn't. Typically, if one person is expressing codependent behaviors, the other partner is as well. They might just be expressing different but complementary behaviors.

Here are a few starter questions to ask yourself:

CODEPENDENCE	HYPER-INDEPENDENCE	INTERDEPENDENCE
Anxious attachment	Avoidant attachment	Secure attachment
Performative	Guarded	Grounded in sense of Self
Loves to be needed	Loves to be desired	Unwilling to externalize self-worth
Sacrifices self to receive love	Struggles to tolerate intimacy	Tends to self first, so they are able to be present/ authentic
Sees potential – wants to "fix"	Sees imperfection – justifies disconnecting	Allows for humanity – each person is their own person
Sees relationship endings as failures/quickly enters new relational dynamics to avoid knowing self	Cynical when relationships end; becomes closed off, reinforcing idea that love isn't real	Looks for lessons – sees each relationship as an opportunity for growth and learning about Self
Values security	Values freedom	Values sovereignty

- Do you feel guilty for speaking up in vulnerable relationships and moments?

- Does it sometimes feel like your feelings and needs don't matter?

- Are you the peacekeeper in many situations? Or were you the peacekeeper growing up?

- Do you find it difficult to say no when someone makes demands on your time and energy?

- Do you tend to hang on to relationships for as long as possible? Even after others would have lost hope?

If you find yourself saying yes to these questions, then follow the thread back and ask yourself the larger question:

Why? Since codependent behaviors are deeply rooted in a fear of abandonment, the questions we need to ask ourselves and the answers we need to try to understand are around what we are trying to avoid feeling or experiencing by *not* showing up authentically. What are we afraid of if we were to show up authentically? If we were to be clear and direct about our needs and desires and boundaries?

We are all wired for attachment in order to survive. If we have a deep-rooted fear that our attachments will be compromised, or will even end, if we speak up, stop caretaking, expect true reciprocity in relationships, communicate clearly, or are just ourselves, then we will choose attachment. Every time.

The Practice

That is, we'll choose attachment—until we don't! Meaning, understanding where the behaviors stem from (which goes much deeper than we can cover in one chapter) is only one piece of the pie. The other piece is to start to show up in a different way. Typically that means doing and saying things in our relationships that make us feel so anxious, fearful, and downright uncomfortable that we want to peel our skin off. That is not an exaggeration. As we mentioned, attachment is one of the most primal needs human beings have in order to survive. If I believe that communicating a boundary or speaking up and being honest with someone about how they hurt my feelings could affect my attachment to them, my internal system literally makes me feel like I'm dying.

So the practice for codependency recovery begins with taking baby steps into that uncomfortable pool of feelings. No one says you have to jump into the deep end. But you do have to do things that don't feel natural to you, and you have to sit with the feelings, process them, breathe into them, journal about and through them. And then repeat. It's only through the process of doing the thing that doesn't feel natural over and over and over again that we can train our nervous system, our brain, and our attachment system to understand that we can do something like express a need and *not die*. Even if the other person doesn't respond well, we still won't die. We might hurt, and we may feel embarrassment and probably shame, but we won't *die*. And little by little, through exposure to those feelings, we begin to increase our tolerance for them.

Think of it like exposure therapy to work through arachnophobia. First, you have to watch videos and look at pictures of spiders. Sitting with that horrible feeling, the hair on your neck stands up, your heart races, and you might even feel sick. Eventually pictures and videos of spiders don't elicit the same response. So then maybe you start to look at actual spiders. You watch them, examine them. Those same horrible feelings come back, over and over again, until they finally lessen. Eventually you might be able to get to the place where you can even hold a spider in your hand without going into a full-blown anxiety spiral. Or not! Maybe you just get to the place where you can tolerate being in the same room with a spider without melting down. That's still progress and shouldn't be minimized!

CHAPTER 14

Fanning the Flames

John

When Vanessa and I first started to get intimate, I asked her if I could slap her while we were making out, about to have sex. She looked at me and very seriously said, "If you slap me, I'm going to slap you back." In that moment, I knew we spoke very different languages in the bedroom.

I like a little kink. She likes long massages. We have different desires and turn-ons, like most people. The textbook solution in this case would be to communicate and explore, meet each other halfway. Tell each other what you like and don't like. You know this. You've probably heard it from your couples therapist. Or read it in a *Psychology Today* article after being frustrated that you had to fake an orgasm yet again.

Here's the truth. It's much more complicated than compromising. Creating intimacy is not like ordering dinner. *Since you got pizza last time, I want Mexican food tonight.* Logically, sure. But we are so much more than logic. We rarely do what makes sense. There are layers to us and our stories. And part of who we are and how we behave is the direct result of conditioning.

Generally speaking, men have been conditioned by porn and locker rooms. I was exposed to graphic images at a very young age. I got my porn stash—basically one ripped picture from a magazine that I would keep under my bed for months—from friends who had older brothers. This was pre-internet, when you had to know people to get porn. I would also watch Cinemax and the Playboy channel in my parents' room while they were at work. These images gave me the first imprint of what sex looked like. I saw men being aggressive. Women enjoying the aggression. I saw penises the size of baby arms. I saw lots of grabbing and pulling and slapping. Sex seemed like a contact sport. I was fascinated and I couldn't get enough. Then, as I got older, the locker-room talk reinforced the idea of sex as a sport. The more women you slept with, the more of a man you were. The bigger your penis, the more of a man you were. All of this conditioned me to believe that sex was tied to manhood. If you weren't having it, you were less of a man. I remember in college I had a friend who was a part of the "100s" club. He had already had sex with over 100 women. I remember how impressed I was, and how I wished I were in that club.

It's no surprise that sex became a shot of dopamine and a scoreboard for me. With addiction in my blood, it was my drug of choice. I used sex for the high, for validation, and for approval, and also to feel better about myself and to be a "man." My wiring and locker rooms distorted healthy sexual intimacy for me. It took years of undoing, dropping into my body, and many cold showers to create new intimate experiences to redefine what healthy sex looks like. Or rather, feels like. I had to erase from my conditioning the pornographic images I was exposed to at an early age. To make sex a full mind and body expression rather than an activity or a way to get my high.

It's still difficult for me today. But I am aware and try to practice presence over performance, executing my new definition of sex rather than trace old blueprints I formed in my early twenties.

Vanessa

I could write an entire book about how the patriarchal structure we live in has screwed up *all* of us in so many ways, one being our ability to deeply and intimately connect in the bedroom, but I won't. Not because I don't have a lot to say, but because a lot of others have already written about it far more eloquently than I ever could. (Read *Untamed* by Glennon Doyle, *Pussy* by Regena Thomashauer, and anything by Esther Perel. If you want to dive headfirst into some very heady depth psychology stuff, read Marion Woodman.)

I have spent most of my life having performative sex. Meaning sex that wasn't about me but about my partner and their ego. About making sure they felt like I was enjoying myself (am I making the right noises at the right time in the right way?), like they were doing a good job (verbal affirmations and more noises), and like they were turned on by me (what positions do I look best in? I'll arch my back this way, let my hair fall that way), and like I was turned on by them. Even if the last thing I wanted to do was be intimate, I would do it anyway, for them and for the relationship.

Having sex this way is fucking exhausting and the opposite of being present and in your body and the experience. This is what women are taught that sex is all about. Their partner's pleasure. Not your pleasure. And God forbid you owned your sexuality or your pleasure during sex. Let the slut shaming commence!

To be fair, I have had partners who truly emphasized my pleasure—it's not like I've only ever had selfish sex—but even in those situations I was still performing in some way or another. So even when I was in a safe sexual encounter and could be present, I still couldn't let myself go. For that reason, I might be able to count on one hand the number of times I truly lost myself in desire, in a sexual experience, or even deeply merged with another person on a soul level during sex (because yes, that's the kind of sex I want). Until I met John.

It's not that our sex life is mind-blowing all the time, or that we're in sync all the time. But I have never once faked an orgasm with him (something that most women, including me, could win an Academy Award for), and I am more able to tell him, without guilt, when I don't want to have sex rather than going ahead and doing it for him. Part of this is John and the emotional safety he provides. Part of this is me and my growth and evolution. And honestly, I'm just older now and don't care as much about fluffing other people's ego pillows. Part of it has been a process of deeply understanding how much patriarchal and puritanical systems have disrupted our erotic connection to Self and to the other. And part of it has come from understanding the biology behind the different types of desire.

DIFFERENT DESIRES

We can give you the textbook answers and tell you to try different things, see a couples sex therapist, sign up for tantra workshops. But the truth is that most people won't do any of that, including us. It's not that we wouldn't, it's just that we haven't . . . yet.

For us, a few different practices help us keep desire alive. The first is an understanding that we have different sex drives, or desires. There are three different types of sexual desire:

- **Spontaneous**—Desire shows up instantly without needing to be stimulated by thought or action

- **Responsive**—Desire shows up in response to both mental and physical stimulation

- **Contextual**—The ability to feel desire is impacted by circumstances and environment

The sex educator and author Emily Nagoski notes that 75 percent of men and 15 percent of women experience spontaneous desire. Five percent of men experience responsive desire, and 35 percent of women. The remaining percentage experience a blend of responsive and contextual desire. So what does this mean for us and, more importantly, for you?

It's crucial to understand your desire type. Coming across

this research for the first time lifted a huge weight off of both our shoulders. Similar to discovering and understanding the other person's love language, knowing your own and your partner's desire types is a way to connect to them deeply and to depersonalize the behavior that is different from your own. While John squarely falls into the spontaneous category and could drop everything and get naked pretty much whenever, Vanessa lives in the blend of responsive and contextual. So while she rarely initiates sex (but not *never*), she enjoys it almost every time. Once the stimulation begins, she remembers that she does enjoy intimacy and connection and needs it to feel connected to herself and to John. Where the depersonalization comes into play is in not beating herself up for not always initiating, or for the times when she is particularly stressed or exhausted or has a million things on her to-do list and truly has no desire to be intimate at all, *and*, on John's part, in not attaching Vanessa's lack of desire in that moment to his self-worth or desirability or the health of the relationship.

The second piece to this puzzle is learning what intimacy and connection look like to each other outside of the bedroom. When John slows down and asks Vanessa questions about herself, her experiences, and her feelings, with genuine curiosity and without any motive other than to know her better, it can feel more stimulating, satisfying, and connecting than an orgasm for Vanessa. When Vanessa opens up and tells John that she desires and appreciates him, and she's specific about why, John feels close to her even if they haven't touched each other yet that day.

It's no surprise that intimacy outside the bedroom also shows up differently for all of us, but exploring and seeking to understand the nuance of your partner's language of desire is yet another way to deepen the connection and meet the need to be seen and understood that we all have as humans. The funny thing about us humans is that, when we feel truly seen, we are more likely to feel truly accepted, and when we feel truly accepted, it is more likely we will feel safe being vulnerable and feel more desire for our partner.

Another really important thing to remember about *all* romantic partnerships is that an ebb and flow in your desire and connectedness is totally normal. You are not going to feel that same heart-skips-a-beat, hair-stands-up-when-they-touch-you way always and forever. Fairy tales and rom-coms have once again done us a major disservice in feeding us the belief that the lead-up to the relationship *is* the relationship. It's not—it's only the lead-up. The relationship is the day-to-day. And sometimes in the day-to-day your connection goes through periods of expansion and periods of contraction.

We need to give ourselves and our relationships a little breathing room in order to grow, to thrive, to expand, to come back together. It's in that coming back together that much of the deeper connection is built. Part of the growth of a connection comes from each person experiencing and growing on their own as well. It can't all be done together, all of the time. We are not saying that you should let stasis in your relationship go on indefinitely, or that you should stay in a place of disconnect over the long term. If it feels uncomfortable for you, name it. If the disconnect feels unsafe to you, name it. If your gut is telling you there is something underneath the distance, name it. There is so much potential for connection in the conversation that could arise from you naming it. Or a painful truth. Either way, that conversation can be liberating. Only you can know what feels good and not so good in your relationship. We're just here to push you to experience and thus tolerate more discomfort and to understand that what we have been taught to believe about what relationships should look and feel like all the time is bullshit.

Questions to Ask Yourself

What are some of the stories you have been conditioned to believe about sex, desire, connection, and intimacy? Where did you learn this stuff? In the moments when you have done exactly what you were "supposed" to do according to what you were told (whether by parents, society, or friends . . . doesn't matter), how did you feel? Did it feel right? Complete? Satisfying? Enough? Which of those stories feels off base for you? Which of them feels like total bullshit when you really sit with it? What would feel more authentic to you? Be honest. If you could have the exact sexual, romantic, intimate experience you desire, what would that look like? Feel like? Sound like?

Can you talk about any of these desires with your partner? Or with someone trusted? Why not? Do you feel shame? Understanding, unwiring, and rewiring our relationship to sex and desire in our relationships starts with questioning the stories we have ingested and then sussing out what is our own desire, our own need, our own fantasy, and what was given to us by an external source. Where can you reclaim more of your truth in this area of your life?

The Practice

We want to talk about a simple and yet profound practice called The Six-Second Kiss by the renowned marriage researcher John Gottman. Let's start with this:

Do you remember your very first kiss? Of course you do. You know exactly where you were and what you were wearing. You remember wondering if you should use your tongue, if your braces would cut her, and how long you should keep your eyes shut. But what you remember the most isn't how it went, but how you felt: the bats in your stomach, the fear in your heart, and your sweaty palms.

Do you remember your 1,547th kiss? Of course you don't. When we kiss someone new, it's exciting. It's our first time experiencing the other person intimately. We take our time, bathe in it, get lost. Our mind is set on discovery mode. We are open to exploring. Once we're in a relationship, kissing becomes routine. The exploration is over. We use kissing as a handshake, a "hi," a "bye," a "see ya later." Or a gateway to other things. Rarely do we kiss to discover. We forget the meaning behind kissing. Kissing is a way to express, connect, validate, assure, give, share, trust, and explore. When's the last time you got so lost in a kiss that you forgot what day it was? When your neck hairs stood up and danced? When the kiss could stand on its own and not need to lead to something more? When nothing mattered but you, the person you were kissing, and that moment?

Gottman recommends the practice of a six-second kiss, twice a day. Why six seconds? Because a six-second kiss has potential. It provides room to be mindful, to experience romance and connection. To feel something. A two-second kiss isn't actually a kiss. It's a peck. A pat on the back. How long are your kisses? What's behind them? Are you kissing just to kiss? Or to actually express your love?

Kiss your partner for six seconds, twice a day. The kisses don't have to be loaded with passion, prompting you guys to call in sick to work so you can have an afternoon delight. It can, and most likely will, feel a bit awkward at first. That's because the two of you aren't used to this practice. That's okay. That's why this is a practice. Make sure it's honest, not forced. And be present. That's all that matters. And, of course, make sure that the kiss is at least six seconds long.

We actually practice this. Maybe you think we're full of shit, but it's true. We really do. Not every single day. But throughout the week one of us will initiate and remind the other to kiss for six seconds. And it works. Because that extra three seconds can remind you of why you are together, why you are both working on building or rebuilding your relationship. It also works as a radar. If there are hurt feelings, if there's resentment, a six-second kiss will bring it to the surface, where both of you will feel it.

CHAPTER 15

Jealousy

We answered a question on social media recently about struggling with jealousy when your partner thinks someone else is "hot." Our answer got a ton of pushback and comments. Jealousy became a controversial topic, opening up insecurity wounds and drawing out heated reactions. It was interesting to explore where these reactions were coming from. Our findings made it clear that our fairy tale of romantic love does a lot of damage to our relationships.

The idea that our partner only fantasizes about us and doesn't notice anyone else (even when masturbating), although seemingly romantic, is not realistic. We are sexual beings. If you're breathing, you have found people attractive and you're going to go on finding people attractive. But that attraction doesn't mean you want to build a relationship with that person, or that you don't love the person you are partnered with. It just means you're human—an animal.

It's denying and rejecting this fact that creates anxiety and control and tugs at your insecurities and fears. Finding out that your partner finds someone else sexy or has fantasized about someone other than you can bring up a ton of tough emotions that have you behaving in unhealthy, controlling, and reactive ways. That only puts cracks in the relationship container, stunts growth, limits trust, and produces drift. It's a common pattern we see all the time, especially in younger couples.

Going through each other's phones. Checking browser histories. Telling your partner what they should and shouldn't wear and how they should and shouldn't behave around the object of desire. All of this unhealthy behavior starts with one thing: denial. Denial that your partner is an individual and a complicated sexual being; denial that they have yet to share and aren't actually obligated to share parts of themselves with you; and denial of the reality that trying to control them, their behavior and thoughts, will not protect you from hurt or perceived emotional danger.

So step one is the opposite of denial. Acceptance. This is the hard part. This is where most people get angry and start throwing around definitions of love and expectations about how people should be in relationships. Now, we are not saying it's okay and healthy to allow yourself to fantasize about someone else every time you and your partner are intimate. We're not saying it's okay to make a comment to your partner every time you notice someone attractive. These kinds of behaviors can actually be red flags. What we're saying is that you and your partner are human. You both have found other people attractive and will keep on finding other people attractive. And you both have at times probably fantasized about someone else, even if only for a moment. That's normal. That's healthy.

Once you both accept that aspect of your humanness, the tension will ease. That's when you can stop taking it so personally and instead pull more from curiosity. When you can start working through your own insecurities and ultimately build a closer bond with each other.

John

I overheard Vanessa and her girlfriend Dené chatting about how they thought Dené's mail carrier was hot. At first I was curious. What did he look like? Why did they think he was so "hot"? When I saw photos of him, I didn't see what all the fuss was about. But the more I continued to hear about how hot he was, the more annoyed I got. I wasn't twenty anymore. I have worked through my jealousy issues. Why was it even bothering me?

Then I realized it wasn't about this one mail carrier. It was an accumulation of Vanessa's mentions over the years of random guys she found attractive. Jared Leto. Lenny Kravitz. "That guy, Steven Yeun, from *The Walking Dead.*" Yeun happens to be Korean, and I'm not sure if that makes it worse or better. But none of these guys looked like me. They were thinner and taller. Much prettier than me.

Then I realized that this was the first relationship I'd been in with a partner who freely expressed who she found attractive. In my other relationships, it was always me. Or my partner would say, "But he's not as hot as you," or something like that to reinforce their attraction to me and make me feel better about myself. Looking back, I see that they were most likely taking care of my ego. Perhaps they were used to the pushback from jealous ex-boyfriends and had learned to not open that can of worms. Or maybe society's giant "shoulds" or their upbringing, telling them how a girlfriend should act, kicked in and they self-corrected according to those standards. Either way, I wasn't used to my girlfriend expressing who she found attractive. This tugged on my insecurities and sometimes caused me to wonder if she was even attracted to me. Even though she frequently said that she was, and I knew that she was, those insecure thoughts hijacked the truth. They can be the virus that spreads and poisons any relationship. But only if you feed it.

Here's the truest truth: Vanessa expresses who she finds attractive because she feels safe with me and believes that I will not get insecure or feel threatened, like previous boyfriends might have. She told me this once as I sank in my seat, checking myself. Here's why it's important to normalize our attraction to others and create a space where the relationship isn't in trouble if we express it: if your partner feels safe enough to express this truth, they will probably feel safe enough to express other truths. This kind of safety produces superglue.

So the next time your partner mentions being attracted to someone, ask yourself: Do I want to build trust or crack it? That will help you with your response.

Vanessa

I have always been very open and honest about the people who I think are attractive. I laugh at how shocked some guys are when they hear women being real in how they talk about sex and specific experiences and "What. I. Would. Do. To. This. Person. If. He. Were. Here. In. Front. Of. Me. Right. Now." There is this misconception that only men are highly sexual and speak this way to their friends. If you ever heard how my friends and I talk about sex and desire, your jaw might drop—though probably not if you're a woman reading this. You probably know exactly what I mean.

Women are supposed to be demure and unwaveringly loyal. We're supposed to be ladies. Ladies don't have sexual fantasies, and they sure as hell don't express them openly to their man. This belief has been planted like a seed, deep in our collective psyche, and those types of toxic seeds are hard to weed out.

In my first relationship we both spoke openly about fantasy and attraction to others, and it felt inviting and stimulating and actually led to hotter sex. In my second relationship my partner wanted to pretend that I was a virgin before him, that I had no other sexual experiences or thoughts that did not revolve around him. To me, this felt stifling and dismissive. As though an entire part of myself was unacceptable and shameful, something not to ever be talked about. It's no surprise that in that relationship I hid many parts of myself and performed in many many ways. It was made clear, even if not verbally, that there were parts of me that could be talked about, accepted, and loved and parts of me that needed to be shut down so as not to upset my partner. If that happened, I would have to clean up and manage and placate.

For me, discussing these topics with my partner helps me understand them more and feel more understood myself. If they get mad or jealous or ask that I not be open about my fantasies, then I know there is something deeper we need to talk about. It is important to me that I am able to express this side of myself, as it is a large part of my authentic identity. It's also important to me that my partner provide a safe and accepting enough space to be open to our talking about this. Not in the sense of rubbing their face in it and expecting them to take it, but instead, accepting that we're both human and each of us is sexual, has desire, and fantasizes.

I'm very aware this is a hot-button topic, and you might not want to explore it with your partner, but what I am prompting you to do here is to explore together issues around desire, insecurity, and societal expectations of both genders. Men aren't the only ones who get jealous and shut down that part of their partner. Women do it too. I've experienced it in my clients and in my female friends. So much of the messaging we get from living in a patriarchal structure is that women's sexuality and sexiness determine their

worth and value as a person. If you admit to finding someone else attractive, or that you're turned on by something in
the bedroom not normally associated with women's desire,
the message is that there is something wrong with you. And
rather than sit with this reaction and examine where it's
coming from, we blame the men for being pigs and sex-
crazed assholes.

Questions to Ask Yourself

When you think about your partner being attracted to another person, what does that bring up in you? Are your
thoughts about your partner being bad or untrustworthy,
for example, or can you go inward and really pinpoint in
yourself what thoughts and emotions are activated by your
partner's attraction to someone else?

Jealousy, like all emotions, is a flag telling you to pay
attention to something deeper. A lack of jealousy can also
be an interesting flag. Feelings of jealousy are completely
normal, but unhealthy behaviors arising from jealousy are
not. So if feelings and thoughts of jealousy do come up,
it might be a good exploration to ask yourself what fears
might underlie those jealous thoughts.

The Practice

Again, we know how activating this topic can be for most
people. We aren't here to question whether that defensiveness or activation is right or wrong, or to tell you that you
should or shouldn't be okay with your partner thinking
someone else is attractive. All we are here to do is give you

jumping-off points for further internal investigation and topics to explore in your relationship as a way to go deeper. If you can tolerate the discomfort that comes up when we communicate about hot topics like this, you're likely to be able to experience more vulnerability and thus more authentic self-expression, with both yourself and your partner.

If you're interested in exploring this topic and have already played around with the "Questions to Ask Yourself" section, the practice then might be asking yourself what turns you on and then communicating that. Focus on *what* you find attractive, not just physically but emotionally, and not so much on *who* you find attractive.

Yes, you will find others attractive. You're human, and there's no need to announce or deny that fact. What should be announced and explored is what you like and what turns you on, then exploring and expanding on the things you find attractive in your partner. Always bringing it back to you and your partner is a great way to use this exploration to go deeper with each other.

CHAPTER 16

Love and Money

Money is one of the top things couples fight about. When they do, though, it's not usually about the money. It's about their relationship with money and how that translates into security and safety. It's about how they define themselves by money. It's about how they were raised, with or without money, and how that experience shaped their shoulds with money. The conflict usually is not about the money itself.

John

The other layer to the "Can I buy the Lucky Charms?" question I used to ask my ex-wife had to do with money. I wasn't making any at that time in my life. She was the breadwinner, and I was the screenwriter, aka starving artist. I defined my worth as a man, in part, by how much money I made. And since I wasn't making any, I didn't feel like I could buy things. I felt like I had to ask her for permission. It was the first time in my life I'd truly felt worth less than my partner.

My parents came to this country with no money. They worked hard and saved to buy a family business—a burger stand—then a fast-food franchise, and then an Italian restaurant turned supper club. Mom and Dad fought too much to work together, so Dad opened a telephone cabling business. And like a traditional Korean family, we (my older brother and I) worked for the family businesses. So we were close to the money. We knew when the family had money, and we knew when we didn't. Money decisions were made by all of us, not just our parents.

This was both good and bad. Good because my brother and I got whatever we wanted. My parents thought being "American" meant designer jeans and sugar cereal. But it was bad because we got whatever we wanted. I didn't truly learn the value of money and how to save it. We weren't rich, but we weren't poor. The pantry was always stocked, and we were always the first kids on the block to have nice things.

Then I married someone who grew up without money. Eating out (fast food) was only for special occasions. There was no family money, so you made your own. I grew up getting mostly whatever I wanted, so when my frugal ex-wife said, "No, we don't need that. Besides, it's bad for you," I'd say, "But why not?" This created tension every time we went grocery shopping. She also thought eating out was a waste of money. I remember the lengths I would go to in order to sneak out and buy myself a cheeseburger. I felt like an addict getting high. Enter shame and feeling like I was not enough.

Our different relationships with money—based on how we were raised and how we defined ourselves by it—became a crowbar in our marriage and caused tension. She saw me as irresponsible and childlike. I saw her as cheap and controlling. For her, it was the first time she was making good money. For me, it was the first time I didn't have any money. We didn't have the tools to communicate, explore, and compromise. We didn't have the ability to understand each other better by examining our stories. Instead, we just held tight to our own side of the tug-of-war rope.

Hanging on to that rope for too long creates resentment, drift, and a change in the chemistry of a relationship. Feelings change. She saw me as her son, not her partner. She felt unsafe. I internalized not making money at the time and defined myself as inadequate and not a "good" husband. So I put more pressure on myself to sell the million-dollar screenplay. That was going to fix everything and finally make me a good husband, and a man. So I slowly lost my life to endless hours of writing in coffee shops, which led to my personal disintegration. I was reeking of desperation. Far from helping my marriage, this helped break it.

This type of pattern is common in many relationships. It's not about the money. It's about your relationship with money, how you define yourself by it, and how that impacts your relationship. It's about safety or feeling a lack of safety. It's about feeling less than or inadequate. It's about the power dynamic. It's about society's shoulds.

Today I don't ask Vanessa if I can buy Lucky Charms. One, she buys Lucky Charms herself. She likes the bad cereal as much as the good-for-you kind. But two, and more importantly, I no longer define myself as a man based on how much money I make. So I don't feel the same shame anymore. Of course, it helps that I am actually making some money these days, unlike in my early thirties. But it's my new relationship with money I have achieved since going on my inner journey, and not allowing myself to be defined by it, that I think really makes the difference in my relationship with Vanessa.

Vanessa

Money is always on my mind. And I mean always. Not like I'm hungry for power and success and getting rich, but more like, do I have enough money to survive? I grew up without a lot of money and also being very aware of how little money we had and what kind of stress that put on my single mother. My relationship with money has had some sort of impact on every serious relationship I've ever had.

Boyfriend number one told me after our relationship went up in flames that he felt emasculated that I made more money in thirty hours of bartending than he made in fifty hours of salaried work in his entry-level music industry job. Boyfriend number two always made less money than I did. We had a lot of overlap in our upbringings with respect to money, but I always had a feeling in that relationship that whoever had the most money had the most power. Hence, when he paid for my yoga teacher training as a "gift," I secretly paid him back by not charging him his half of certain utilities until we were even. I never told him. Healthy, I know.

Boyfriend number three didn't seem to have much ambition to do or accomplish more than his relatively low-paying desk job. He was in his late thirties and still lived with a roommate in an apartment. Judging him the way I did was not my finest hour, but I did a lot of work around the understanding that the source of my judgment was my need to feel safe and secure and my unhealthy desire to work myself to death to hoard "enough" money (it would never be enough money). He was happy where he was at in his life, and that should have been all that mattered.

And then came boyfriend number four—John. When I met him, I was making a career transition and living on student loans. He was getting traction in his career and had just landed his second book deal. He gave freely and never made me feel like he held money over my head. But I held it over my head myself. I demanded to pay half of everything, always.

Then I got pregnant. And as the pregnancy developed, so did my crippling anxiety around money. I worked for myself, and I had no maternity leave (not that we really get much in the US anyway). I had no savings because I had used it all while interning as a therapist. I physically wouldn't be able to work for a period of time. I was in therapy at the time and continued throughout the pregnancy. Probably 80 percent of what we talked about at that time was my fear around security and my relationship with money. I spun, a lot. I asked John to help me make spreadsheets so I knew exactly what our incoming and outgoing looked like. I calculated the earliest point I could go back to work so I could contribute financially. And through it all, my therapist and John reminded me that it was impossible to put a price tag on what I was about to be doing and bringing into the partnership (i.e., birthing and keeping a child alive). I shrugged that off. Until it happened. Until I physically and mentally couldn't do anything other than eat, nap, and feed the baby.

I'll give you a synopsis of what I learned in therapy, in hopes that it might help you go deeper in your self-understanding too:

I had spent a lifetime in fight-or-flight mode around financial security, so feeling secure about "having enough" was an absolutely foreign concept to me and my nervous system. I didn't trust the feeling, and so I didn't trust my partner.

I tied my worth as a strong woman to how much I was contributing financially. I had always taken care of myself, and it made me feel weak to allow myself to be provided for financially.

In the back of my mind I had a belief that all relationships end, and that men always leave (whether physically or emotionally or both). So you have to make sure you're able to provide for yourself and don't end up destitute when he does.

And here are some of the ways in which I have grown and softened around this topic through the relationship John and I have built:

Living in a state of panic is unhealthy for everyone involved. It robs us of our ability to be present and find joy in our lives. That's not to say there isn't money stress and sometimes it's more consuming than at other times (I know, I grew up without much money), but when we stay in a state of stress all the time, we truly miss out on life. I've had to develop a strong mindfulness practice for those times when my nervous system gets activated and I go into fight-or-flight. Because if it's activated in one part of my life, the stress trickles into all of them. Notice. Breathe. Repeat.

My worth is found in so much more than my income. I do a *lot* for those in my life, especially for John and Logan, and that is invaluable.

When I am in a state of "mine and yours" versus "ours," I am walled off, defensive, and hard. This makes it impossible for me to soften into the vulnerability required by the type of relationship I truly crave.

And none of these revelations make me any less capable or competent.

Questions to Ask Yourself

What was your parents' relationship with money? Did you grow up with or without it? What was the impact of that on you growing up? What is your current relationship with money? Do you feel it's healthy or unhealthy, and why? Do you feel you are worth more as a person when you have more money? Do you view others differently depending on how much money they have? How has your relationship with money impacted your relationships? How do you wish you felt or engaged with money differently? How would making that change impact your relationship?

The Practice

The point of a lot of the practice for this topic is to understand yourself through deep questioning. For most of us, our relationship with money runs deep and branches out into many areas of our life—such as how and when you feel safest, what factors for you into having a strong sense of Self and self-esteem, and whether you have a high threshold for the anxiety that comes from the unknown. There are a lot of courses and coaches out there specializing in helping people improve their relationship with money, and that may feel like something helpful to explore.

If you have a good base of knowledge of yourself when it comes to money and are ready to have some conversations with your partner, start with sharing your findings. Maybe some revelations about yourself that came from digging deeper. Then make a commitment to continue to revisit the topic as it comes up. Because it will. Money comes and goes as our life circumstances change. Having a kid, buying a house, needing an unexpected surgery, needing to financially take care of a loved one, starting a new business, losing a job, retirement—all of these have an impact on our relationship with money. An endless number of potential events will keep you noticing any discomfort you have with money and give you a chance to use that discomfort as a prompt to peel back another layer of the onion.

CHAPTER 17

What If You're Not Feeling It Anymore?

Many people believe that if you're not feeling it anymore in your relationship, there is clearly something wrong. They assume that the relationship has died. It has run its course, and there's nothing you can do. It's time to sit down and have the "it's not you, it's me" conversation. So you break up, go on your "single on purpose" journey as you connect back to you, then meet someone who makes you feel alive again. It's powerful and dreamy and you realize you were right. It was time for that last relationship to expire, because this new one gives you butterflies instead of bats. Until things get hard. But you stay in it and swim past the breakers. And things get better.

But even then, you get to a confusing place where you're not feeling it anymore. Again.

Here's the truth. In any relationship, you're not going to feel it anymore at some point. Even if things are good and no one's fighting. Even if you still get along great. Even if there is no anger, resentment, or eggshells. The longer you do life with someone, the higher the chance of natural drift and growing apart. This is the natural default. You are human, which means you are wired to be curious and ever evolving. Drift and doubt come with the human package. They are baked in. Also, relationships take a shit ton of work. You may just be exhausted. This doesn't mean you want to invest in someone else, or that you should. It just means you're human.

One of the most damaging misconceptions about relationships is that you should *always* be feeling it. That love and attraction is a constant and if things dip for no apparent reason, that's a sign that something is wrong. Yes, it could be. But it could also just be that things get boring and stale like a bag of chips left open. Sorry if that just made your face cringe, but that's real life. It's not the rom-com movie trailer we constantly play in our head and compare our relationship to. That's called programming. And it's unfair.

The reason why relationships are not a constant is because *we* are not a constant. We go through our own inner journeys. Daily. Besides external factors like pressure and anxiety from work, the direction of our career, our relationships with friends and family, parenting, investing in hobbies and passions, there are also internal factors, like our relationship with ourselves. One day we really like our-selves, who we are and what we're doing, and the next day we don't. Drift and "not feeling it" can come from our relationship with Self, not just from our relationship with our partner. There is an ebb and flow within each of us that directly impacts our relationship with others, especially our partner. And since we are two people (assuming we're in a monogamous relationship of two) who are each going through the ebbs and flows of our own internal journey, there's going to be distance at times. If this distance goes on for long stretches, one or both of us can start having the feeling of not feeling it anymore.

If we don't come back from that—if one of us ebbs while the other flows—and we both stay at that distance for too long without checking in (doing life alone), then yes, not feeling it anymore can become legit. Both people can drift too far to turn back and come together again, and feelings start to permanently change. But if we are both aware and we both respect and support each other's ebb and flow, while continuing to hold hands, look each other in the eyes, and check in, drift and doubt can be totally normal and healthy. These periods can actually serve as a love rubber band that snaps us back closer together after being stretched, deepening the relationship.

John

I'm not sure at what point I stopped feeling it. It wasn't like I woke up one day and it hit me in the face like a back-handed slap. It wasn't a knowing in my soul. It was more of a slow burn. A stirring. A coming to. And of course it was normal. I knew there were going to be points in the relationship when I wasn't feeling it. But the thing is, I didn't do anything about it. I didn't acknowledge it. I didn't explore or investigate to see how much of that feeling had to do with me and not my partner or the relationship. I just let it smolder until the entire house was on fire. Until there was nothing left to do but run. Twice. Yes, I ran from two long-term relationships.

When I look back today, I realize there is a pattern in my life. I tend to run after about three years. I don't "do the work," as they say. I allow myself to drift and fantasize. I start to pick apart my partner and the relationship and ultimately convince myself that it has expired. I tell myself we have grown apart and that it's unfixable. It's a way of hiding and not facing hard things. It's what I'm famous for at parties—slipping out the back without saying a proper goodbye.

I know this is a pattern because I have felt it come up with Vanessa. It's not as strong as a triggering parent when you go back home for the holidays. But it's there, like a weathered carving of your name in a tree. And guess how long Vanessa and I had been together when it first came up? You guessed it—three years. But it's different this time. I am aware of it. But more importantly, I'm not afraid of it. I have more understanding of myself today. I'm no longer a walking reaction. I know where old patterns lead.

Also, what Vanessa and I have built is different from what I built with anyone else. The space is different. Our dynamic is different. We are both different from when we were with others in the past.

Love is making a choice every single day to either love or not love. That's it. It's that simple. Either to continue the process or not. We fall in and out of love. We feel it, then we don't. This ebb and flow doesn't mean we don't love the person. But it leaves us with a choice. There is a difference between feeling love for someone (caring about them) and loving someone (choosing to love them). We may feel love for someone forever, but that doesn't mean we choose to love that person forever. The choice to love is not a feeling—it is an action. That is why it is so difficult. Love requires us to do something. Sometimes it is easy to love. Sometimes it is extremely difficult. And sometimes it has more to do with us than the person we love. But at the end of the day, it's always a choice.

Although love varies, it also deepens. The longer we stay on that journey we've embarked on together, the more fruit the process will bear. Our investment will pay off. Our choices will become easier. We will become stronger not only as a couple but also as individuals, *assuming the love process is healthy*—i.e., we are both doing the work. The choice to love creates an opportunity to hit notes in life that we could never hit alone, and this is what makes our choice worth it.

Vanessa

I don't have a three-year-itch pattern like John, maybe because I can lean more avoidant. I can feel really at ease in the contraction pattern in a relationship. Almost more at ease than in the expansion phase. Having space to breathe and be alone and not feel the pressure of being intimate or vulnerable can feel like a warm blanket. Unfortunately, it can also be a heavy wet blanket that keeps us stuck and unmoving.

While John has the pattern of drifting and then bailing after three years, I have the pattern of staying in things far too long because I'm comfortable in the drift and the distance. The beautiful thing about our relationship that feels different for me from past relationships is that John expects a lot from me. Not in a bad way, but in a "Hey, I'm in this too, and I'm doing work too, and I expect you to show up and give this your all and not phone it in" type of way. I've never had someone challenge me in the way John does. He checks my distance. He reminds me that the relationship and what we are building is greater than the two of us as individuals. He reminds me that a conscious relationship is what I want too, even when it feels like a lot of work and I would rather just phone it in and nap. He challenges me, on the daily, to choose love instead of choosing the comfort of distance.

> **Conscious relationship:** A relationship in which both participants are committed to growth and evolution to develop a stronger sense of Self, higher emotional intelligence, an increasing capacity to self-soothe, and stronger communication.

Questions to Ask Yourself

If you're not feeling it anymore, explore your own inner journey. What are you going through right now? Is there something happening in your life that's disconnecting you from yourself and the relationship? Are you in your head? Did an ex call, triggering something? Are you anxious about your work or your career? Is family life stressful and over-whelming? Are you generally not happy because things aren't going your way? Are you holding on to anger or re-sentment? If so, what are you doing to work through this? Reading self-help books and trying to sort it out yourself is great, but not enough. It's really helpful to process stress and anxiety with someone who can see you better than you can see yourself, preferably a therapist or relationship coach.

If it's not you, is it your partner or the relationship? If it is, what is the problem? What's happening that needs to be resolved or worked through? What do you need to express to your partner to get this going? What are you afraid of ad-mitting or expressing to them? Or is it something more like not having enough quality time with your partner? Have both of you gotten too busy? Maybe you need connection and romance? Express your need without blame. Be spe-cific, and try new ways of connecting. Approach it like you are on the same team, strategizing for the win. Because you are.

The Practice

Some of us have a tendency to bail when the going gets tough. Others have a tendency to hold on to things much longer than they should. This chapter can't address all of the nuances of not feeling it anymore, but what we hope to provide you with is a spark of curiosity as well as tools and insights that you might not have considered yet. Also, just reading the rest of this book could be one giant practice if you aren't feeling it anymore. The most important thing to remember, however, is that you are only 50 percent of the relationship. You can only be responsible for yourself and how you show up. How your partner shows up and the amount of effort they put in is entirely on them.

Conclusion: Filling Your Jar

John

After going to therapy school, helping thousands with their relationships, and doing my own inner work, I still don't have all the answers. There is no color-by-numbers advice when it comes to love and relationships. And as much as you have learned and grown from your previous love experiences, there are always new problems and challenges. Because love is not a constant. It is its own living, breathing thing, always changing and evolving like you are. And no matter how many tools you have today, every new relationship has its own dynamic, its own emotional activations and triggers, and its own traps and mirrors.

The greatest thing I've learned about relationships is that they are meant to have turbulence. One of the most common misconceptions about love is that it's supposed to be easy. And that if it's not, you're with the wrong person. The truth is that relationships are hard. They're supposed to be. That's how we learn, grow, and evolve. There must be a journey. You have to go somewhere and come back. The difference between a healthy relationship and an unhealthy one is that you don't come back in an unhealthy one. You just leave the village. And eventually get lost. The coming back again and again is what healthy looks like. That journey is what produces trust and a stronger bond, but also, more importantly, revelations and inner growth. Without this journey, there is no story. And without a story, there is no life.

We all know that building healthy relationships is one of the hardest things to do in this life. It's hard not just because it takes compromise and commitment, but also because self-understanding is the fuel needed to keep a relationship growing or it will die. And to understand Self, we have to look inward, be honest with ourselves, and take ownership. Loving someone brings up things in us we may not want to look at. Building a relationship with that person is not just a decision. It's a journey that requires patience, dissolving of ego, and a break with patterns that are wired deep in us. To love someone requires continually doing a self-inventory. If we don't do that work, it won't be healthy love. It will be two people bouncing on and off each other instead of evolving with each other. And the higher notes of love will not be hit.

Therefore, there is a great responsibility in loving someone. It is a daily choice and sometimes a fight—with your old self. Otherwise, the ship goes down. What makes loving someone so hard? The continuous tearing down and rebuilding of your relationship with *yourself*. This is why so many people leave relationships. This is the hard part. But what in life of value isn't hard?

There will be days when you and your partner won't be able to stand each other. There will be days when you will want to take the long way home. You will disagree on things, like movies and books and politics and dinner. He will forget things. You will run late. Your friends will have opinions. You will fight. Maybe a lot. You will shut down. He will wonder. But at the end of the day you will both come back—to each other. And no matter how many times you fight, you will always fight fair. That will be the non-negotiable. And you will be together knowing that you are choosing to be together. Not because of logic or loneliness or a ticking clock. Not because you look good on paper, take cute photos, or think you'll make cute babies. Not because you've already committed to the relationship. Not because you don't want to be alone. But because you believe in what you are building and you're making a choice, every single day, to be in this and love each other the best way you both know how. Your relationship will not be built on fear, as many are, but on courage and transparency. And like any relationship, there will be no guarantee.

You will not compare this to what was. Any residue you have from previous relationships you will work on individually. It is your own responsibility. Both of you taking responsibility for your own previous experience is what being in something healthy looks like. You and your partner will sharpen each other; you will make him feel beautiful, and he will make you feel invincible and vice versa. The only thing you can promise is to be honest and to love as hard as you can. Without losing yourself. Both of you know there is risk. Both of you know people can get hurt. But both of you are willing to put that on the line to experience the high notes of something meaningful and greater than self. You will each take responsibility for your own shit, but together you will also settle for nothing less than creating a space for magic.

Vanessa

Taking almost everything I have learned, and am continuing to learn, about relationships and putting each topic into a two- to five-page chapter was incredibly difficult. Relationships and people are nuanced and complicated, and it's that nuance that makes us so beautiful and unique. But what I have learned as a therapist is that there are dysfunctional patterns that many of us fall prey to. These patterns almost always serve the same purpose—to protect us from feeling hurt.

These patterns can be reshaped into something incredible by understanding the reasons for them, realizing that we are not alone in falling into them, and then challenging ourselves to do things that feel very different from what we are used to. That something incredible, to me, is a romantic partnership that feels at once accepting *and* challenging. That feels safe and also a little dangerous. That feels boring and exhilarating, expansive and grounded. So far, I have found that in John.

I don't feel butterflies every time I look at John, or feel like I'm in the flow with him every day. Some days we are truly like ships passing in the night. But I choose to love him, every day. And when I get a little too self-involved and forget to choose him, he reminds me what that feels like on his end. Then I practice understanding before being understood. I stretch myself and talk about things that make me uncomfortable, because choosing comfort over growth is no longer appealing to me.

Like everyone, I am a messy and imperfect human just figuring it out as I go. But I am also committed to showing up in my messiness and sharing what I have learned, through my own personal journey and through the themes and stories of the people who trust me with their inner worlds. We might all be nuanced as beings, but we are also very similar in our desire for connection and deeply fulfilling attachment. If nothing else, I am committed to challenging people to think differently about what they know about themselves and about relationships and to continue to create a community of people who are on the same journey and who want more for themselves, their relationships, and thus the world. Yes, the world.

What we see in the world, the collective, is simply a reflection of what we see at home. The more people commit to going inward, practicing self-compassion and challenging themselves to love in the best and most expansive way they possibly can, it is only natural that the dynamic of the world will change too. We will be healthier partners, healthier parents, healthier employees, and healthier global citizens. So know that you aren't just stretching yourself and challenging yourself for yourself alone. You're doing it for everyone. No pressure.

Acknowledgments

Vanessa

I'm grateful in general, to so many, and in particular to a specific few.

Thank you to Laura Yorke and Hillary Swanson for taking a chance on me, and to Sydney Rogers for pushing this book until it truly sang. I believe it's something we can all be proud of and will be, forever!

Thank you to Ashley Torrent for being my gateway . . . to everything. To understanding, to healing, to Pacifica, to my Self. Without you, I don't know if any of this, of me, would be here as it is today.

Thank you to my past relationships for loving me the best you could and for allowing me an opportunity to peel layers and learn about myself in ways I could never have done without you as my mirror.

And finally, thank you to my mother for keeping the ship afloat at all costs, for teaching me how to love ferociously, for giving me my voice and my sass, and for nurturing my curiosity and an unquenchable thirst to stand up for what I think is right.

John

So grateful to Laura Yorke for answering my query letter years ago and selling the shit out of me. You've opened doors to parts of me I had locked away when I stamped myself a failed screenwriter.

Thank you Hilary Swanson, not only for all the at-bats you have given me (three to be exact), but also for being in the stands—your friendship. You've been a guide and a mentor and I am glad you're in my life.

Thank you Sydney Roger for running with this kite—championing this book. For your guidance, your laser eye, and for believing that love can be healthy. And also rebuilt. We could not have gotten this in the sky without you.

To anyone who has bought my other books, follows me on social, listens to my ramblings on my podcast, or gets my texts, thank you a thousand times. You have given my life meaning and purpose, something I didn't have before I met you.

Appendix 1

Love Lessons (in a Shot Glass)

Like you, we have been in many long-term relationships, short-term relationships, and long-distance relationships, done lots of dating and situationships, and gone through stretches of no dating. We've been in fulfilling relationships and not so fulfilling relationships, and we've been catfished, rejected, confused, present, in our heads, open, narrow, and conflicted. We have loved addicts, been codependent, and struggled through many of our own issues (and continue to). Through this journey, we've had some revelations. Here are ten of our greatest love lessons. We made them short and to the point so they don't drag on and confuse you.

1. **Love is not a battlefield. Your head is.**
    Yes, love can feel like tiptoeing through a forest of explosives, and that's probably what Pat Benatar was

feeling when she wrote the song. But ultimately it's everything in between our ears—our thinking, wiring, definitions, triggers, insecurities, beliefs about ourselves, all formed from our story, which includes previous love experiences—that makes love feel that way. The destruction is real, but where it comes from is not love itself. It comes from us. Toxicity doesn't come from love—it comes from a lack of self-awareness and tools and from the dynamic of the relationship. Jealousy doesn't come from love—it comes from our own insecurities. Jumping to conclusions and making assumptions based on feelings instead of facts doesn't come from love—it comes from our cognitive distortions.

Love is not a battlefield. Your head is. If not your head, then the other person's head. Or both. It's what's happening in our heads that creates the feeling that we're in a war zone. Be aware of your thought patterns and question what's truth, what's distortion, and what's residue from your past.

2.   There is no such thing as perfect.
We all want the perfect partner. If that's your end game, you're going to be playing the game forever. No one is perfect, and you know this. But we keep searching for perfection, and it makes us judge and dismiss people and accumulate a lot of what-ifs. We've learned to toss all our definitions, labels, and what we think "perfect" looks like. Letting go of "perfect" will give you your ocean back. Otherwise, you'll just keep fishing in a small plastic swimming pool.

Yes, we have certain types that we gravitate toward. But it's important to be open. Chasing "perfect" will only give you the same experiences, because your definition of "perfect" won't change. It's the same one we've been clutching onto since college. It's time to toss that shit. There is no growth or evolution in the same experiences. Give yourself a new experience by deleting "perfect" from your vocab. You are looking for something you haven't been attracted to before. You are looking for new, fresh, different. Because in that window there is learning and revelations and discovery. That's what love is about. The new. Not the repeated.

3. **Dating can be fun.**
Put the tomatoes down. Overall, yes, dating sucks. We agree. But it can be fun. Really. It's possible. We've been there. It happened to us! Dating can be fun with the right mindset. The greatest mistake people make with the dating process is having expectations. We meet or swipe or DM or FaceTime someone, and suddenly we're filling in a lot of blanks and imagining what they're like, what they would be like in a relationship, in bed, around our friends. We're just setting ourselves up for disappointment.

Expectations create giant cliffs that you will fall from if they are not met. And chances are, they will not be met. So instead of having expectations, focus solely on the excitement of meeting a new person, hearing a new story, trying a new restaurant, seeing a new museum, movie, or whatever, and if there's chemistry and attraction, that's extra. If not, just have a good fucking time. Be grateful that someone wants to get to know you and spend time with you. Dating is not about finding your soulmate. Dating is about hearing new stories and having new experiences. Detach everything else.

4. **If someone is unsure about you, it's never worth the investment.**

Relationships are hard enough. If you have to convince someone to be with you, what do you think that would look like? When someone is unsure about us, we naturally want to convince them to want us because that would mean we are worthy. We are wanted. We have value. But we're not thinking about what the relationship would look like. We'll tell you. It will be short-lived. We've both learned to stop chasing people. It never works out. One person is constantly seeking approval and validation while the other is getting bored. It burns out like a candle. Instead, make it clear that you'll meet the other person only halfway, until you build something together, and then you'll swim the ocean with them. Don't try to build something on ambivalence.

5. **Love is peeling an onion, not biting an apple.**

The first layer is not love. It's infatuation. Skin. Lust. Connection. Chemistry. Butterflies. All the possibilities of what something could be. Love doesn't happen until the layers are peeled away. Until you see all of someone's layers and accept them, embrace them, and choose to love them.

We're all looking for lightning in the bottle, the "you just know" feeling. But feelings alone don't build healthy, lasting, meaningful relationships. We have powerful connections with certain people, and that's great. That means something. But more and more needs to be discovered. A sustainable relationship takes more than eyes meeting across the room.

Love is about peeling away our layers together by experiencing each other as whole persons, not just as parts of ourselves. Love is leaning into life's shitstorms together, hands locked, learning, growing, fighting resistance and triggers, and sharpening each other along the way.

6. **If someone wants to be with you, you will know.**
So many people make excuses for why they can't be in a relationship, and those reasons may be valid. But we've learned that if someone really wants to be with you, they'll toss everything else out the window. We're not referring to people making a strong, healthy decision to not pursue toxic relationships. That is a good thing and happens often. We're talking about people who say they want to be with you but make a shit ton of excuses for why they can't be, like, "I'm not ready for a relationship."

Okay, fine, but even if you're not ready for a relationship, you still won't cut off a person if you're truly into them. We all want love and know how rare connections are. So we go in the water, even if we're scared or "not ready," because logic always takes a backseat when it comes to love. And yes, fear of intimacy is a real thing and people sabotage relationships all the time. We get afraid. We second-guess. We hesitate. But if someone's really into you, you will know. They will make some kind of effort. They will try. They will communicate. They will not run or hide or ghost. The next time someone says, "I'm not ready," be aware that what they're really saying is, "I'm not that into you."

7. **No one's ever really "ready" for a relationship.**

Relationships are like having children. You'll never truly be ready. You just do it and make things work when you feel it. What does being "ready" for a relationship look like anyway? Self-help books, relationship articles, and seminars have created this false image of what your internal life should look like before you decide to love someone. The truth is, you don't know when you're going to meet someone who blows your knee-high socks off. Or maybe someone you already know who you suddenly see differently and have romantic feelings for. And from what we both know about life, it comes when you least expect it—when you're not "ready." So what do you do—turn down a chance at love because you read somewhere you need to be at a certain place to love right? People are dynamic, always changing, evolving, learning, going through shit, falling down, getting up, getting hurt, healing, letting go, moving on. There is no such thing as ready, because you'll never be perfect. So just love as hard as you can with what you have. Like our parents did and their parents did.

Yes, the more you invest in yourself, the more you bring to the table. But that is an ongoing process that never stops. So ready doesn't exist. Love is a carousel you jump on when you see the horse you want to jump on.

8. Hold love. Don't grab it.

We love the metaphor of holding love like you would sand, with two open hands, and we remind ourselves of it when we approach relationships. Many grab love, and then it slips from their hands. Behind grabbing is control and blueprints and definitions and judgment. People think grabbing love is what it means to love hard, but the opposite is true. Think about love as a bird you're trying to feed. Chase the bird and it will always fly away. The more you try to grab it, the faster it will flee. But if you just hold the food out, the bird will come to you. And the more it trusts you, the more frequently it will come. Love is the same. It is not something to be grabbed. Love is about holding space. And in that space, it grows. Grabbing love will always prevent growth. It sets off our fight-or-flight response. It breaks trust. It makes people flee.

Hold love.

Don't grab it.

9. You can always love harder.

First, you have to define what "harder" looks like for you. Loving harder doesn't necessarily mean caring about someone more. Loving harder may mean giving someone more space. Loving harder may mean looking at yourself and your unhealthy patterns. Loving harder may mean acceptance. Loving harder may mean working on yourself. Loving harder may mean letting go and walking away. Loving harder may mean not giving up.

Ask yourself what loving harder looks like to you. A good place to start is to ask yourself whether you're giving or taking. Many believe they are giving when they are actually taking. If you are using love to make yourself feel better, you are taking. If you are using love to control someone, you are taking. If you are using love to fill holes in yourself, you are taking. Giving is sharing yourself with someone. Giving is coming in as a whole person. Giving is always looking inward first. Giving is accepting someone for who they are and championing their story.

10. **Don't stop believing (be Journey).**
We've all been rejected. We've all been hurt. We've all had our hearts shattered. We've all been in things that ended unexpectedly, that made no sense. We've been cheated on. Manipulated. Left. After a while, these experiences can catch up with us and cause us to stop believing in love, like we stop believing in Santa Claus. Or we come to think of love as a very hot stove we choose to stay away from.

But here's the thing. What we believe will be the rudder determining where we will go, not just with love but with everything. Our beliefs determine our experiences. So if we stop believing in our ideal love, we will never experience the kind of love we dream about. Love will just be an idea. A billboard. A commercial.

So we must continue to believe, with every fiber of our being. If we all stopped believing, love would become extinct and we would all just become empty soda cans. We have to keep believing, if not for ourselves, then for everyone else.

Life is about love.

And love is what teaches us how to live.

Appendix 2

A simple but powerful exercise we sometimes do with our clients is have them write a letter to their exes. It's not meant to be sent. It's meant to help our clients get their feelings out, to reflect, and possibly take ownership in some way. Putting pen to paper can be very therapeutic. Dumping out jumbled thoughts and feelings like a 10,000-piece jigsaw puzzle, then putting the pieces together to form a clearer picture. The beat taken to organize thoughts and feelings creates a space for revelations, insights, and forgiveness—forgiveness for themselves as well as the exes. It helps to let go.

We've both done this exercise. Here are our letters to our exes.

A Letter to My Exes: Vanessa

I want to say first that I'm sorry. I'm sorry I wasn't aware of my patterns. I wasn't aware of how my unconscious and your unconscious were locked in an unseen battle to heal wounds that could never be healed, not with each other. I'm sorry that I stewed in resentment rather than speaking up in a healthy and clear way. That I loved you for the potential of who I thought you could be rather than for who you were in the moment. That my unexamined attachment wounds caused me to withdraw and emotionally abandon you every time I was overwhelmed or afraid. That I wasn't aware of how I was loving with my past. That I wasn't able to communicate my needs in a way that didn't feel like I was nagging or mothering you. That I mothered you. That my codependency caused me to use emotions and words to try to manipulate and control in order to soothe my own anxieties. That my fear of rocking the boat was greater than my desire to be authentic and truthful about my feelings. That my abandonment wound ran so deep that it controlled my ability to be truly vulnerable with you, and that, in the end, we could never truly be in it 100 percent because I just wasn't capable. I'm sorry if my inability made it feel unsafe for you to go there as well.

I also want to say thank you. Thank you for loving me the best way that you knew how. Thank you for all of the laughs we shared and the amazing memories and experiences I now hold close. Thank you for helping me understand myself more fully and for being a part of my journey. Thank you for supporting me and encouraging me. And honestly, thank you for the conflict. It was more helpful for me than you will ever know.

Please know that I fully own my part in the souring of the relationship. I will not slander your name or play the victim. I also will not take on more than my 50 percent of the responsibility, as it is not mine to carry, and taking on more than my share would rob you of your ownership—should you choose to hold it.

I love you and I want the best and most amazing life possible for you. I hope that you find or have found a depth of love and acceptance that you never imagined possible, and I hope that you reflect back on our time together with some fondness. I hope that you know I loved you fiercely, in the absolute best way I could.

Love,
Vanessa

A Letter to My Exes: John

These messages are scattered like puzzle pieces, unnamed, unidentified, and in no particular order. They are snippets of my feels and what I would say to my exes today if I could.

To my first real relationship, I look back at our dance and feel nothing but gratitude. When you wanted to end it, I was sad, but it felt right. I remember playing

Green Day's "Good Riddance" while driving my mom's champagne Cadillac and having a sense of acceptance and closure. When we ran into each other a decade later at the Al-Anon meeting and you confessed that you had kissed someone at a concert while we were together, I wasn't mad or hurt. It just made me realize that people drift and that three years is a long time. You were the first girlfriend who slept in my room, laying tracks for my parents to accept me dating non-Korean girls. Our love was innocent and genuine. I'm so grateful you were my relationship training wheels, and when I think about you, I only see the light in your smile. *"It's something unpredictable. But in the end it's right. I hope you had the time of your life."*

Oregon, your last email was crushing. It was extremely hurtful and confusing. I thought we were good, but then realized you're still not. I had no idea how much anger and resentment you still carry for what happened, especially after ten years of radio silence when we finally sat down and you gave me the kind of goodbye hug that felt like things were closed for you and you genuinely wanted the best for me. I guess it's fair. I have tried to put myself in your shoes. I could blame what happened on so many things—my wiring, codependency, addiction in my blood, being a child, and not having a sense of self—but at the end of the day I was aggressive and dishonest with you. I'm sorry for hurting you the way I did, in so many ways. If there was one thing I could go back and change in this life, it would be what happened between us. I hope you and your family are well and thriving. I will always love you guys, from a distance.

Georgia, you were a soft sparrow I held with two hands. Then stepped on. You trusted me, and I was careless and reckless with your heart. I didn't know I was going to end it the way I did. I am sorry if I made you feel insecure and unlovable. Or maybe you realized that you dodged a bullet. I remember you said to me once, "You're not happy." And I remember being defensive. But you were right. I wasn't happy. And I wonder how much of that contributed to my drift with us. Thank you for being so kind and gentle with me. You made me feel like I hung the moon. Saying sorry doesn't change anything, so I just want you to know that you had a huge impact on my life and our collision was a reminder of what I needed to work on.

Florida, I'm going to focus on what we had. Not on how things went down. You got me in a way no one else did. I always think about two kids ditching school and getting into things when I think about our relationship. It makes sense since we had a friendship base. Or maybe we were childhood friends in a past life. We built a fort and played hard. And I will always value that. As well as our story and who I've become because of it. I have no idea where you're at today with me. But I hope there is no hate or resentment. I have zero on my end. Only good thoughts and best wishes for your trajectory.

Love,
John

About the Authors

JOHN KIM, LMFT, aka The Angry Therapist, practices complete authenticity and transparency with his many clients, an approach frowned upon in the traditional clinical world, and continues to look for new and unconventional ways to help people. He believes, "If we're going to talk about life, let's do life while we're talking." He writes books, sends daily texts to thousands, and documents his journey on his popular podcast, *The Angry Therapist*.

VANESSA BENNETT, LMFT, is a holistic psychotherapist and codependency expert. Her therapeutic approach integrates years of study in depth, Buddhist, and yoga psychology. She cohosts the *Cheaper Than Therapy* podcast and leads retreats and workshops dedicated to helping people break habits of self-abandonment and instead choose inner belonging.